THE VAMPIRE
DEFANGED

THE VAMPIRE DEFANGED

HOW THE EMBODIMENT OF EVIL BECAME A ROMANTIC HERO

Susannah Clements

BrazosPress
a division of Baker Publishing Group
Grand Rapids, Michigan

Published by Brazos Press
a division of Baker Publishing Group
P.O. Box 6287, Grand Rapids, MI 49516-6287
www.brazospress.com

Printed in the United States of America

Library of Congress Cataloging-in-Publication Data
Clements, Susannah, 1974–
      The vampire defanged : how the embodiment of evil became a romantic
hero / Susannah Clements.
         p.   cm.
      Includes bibliographical references (p.   ) and index.
      ISBN 978-1-58743-289-7 (pbk.)
      1. Vampires in literature. 2. Vampire films—History and criticism. 3. Vam-
pires on television. I. Title.
PN56.V3C54 2011
809′.93375—dc22   2010043664

11   12   13   14   15   16   17   7   6   5   4   3   2   1

Contents

1. Why Vampires Matter   1
2. Bram Stoker's *Dracula*: Sin and the Power of the Cross   13
3. Anne Rice's Vampire Chronicles: Eternal Guilt and Transcendent Love   33
4. *Buffy the Vampire Slayer*: Sin and Sacrifice, Postmodern Style   57
5. Sookie Stackhouse: Sex and the Socialized Vampire   81
6. Stephenie Meyer's Twilight Saga: The Vampire as Teenage Heartthrob   103
7. Vampire Sinners   125
8. Vampire Saviors   141

Conclusion   161
Timeline of Referenced Vampire Texts   165
Notes   167
Bibliography   183
Index   193
Acknowledgments   199

1

Why Vampires Matter

I don't think Jesus would mind if somebody was a vampire.

Sookie in "First Taste" (*True Blood*, season 1)

The vampire is a hit.

In 2009, "Twilight Parties" were held around the world to celebrate the midnight DVD release of the film based on Stephenie Meyer's young adult vampire novel. Teens, "tweens," and adults gathered in living rooms, bookstores, and funeral homes to watch *Twilight* by candlelight, drink blood-red punch, and use napkins secured by plastic vampire-teeth rings. Once a creature from our nightmares, the vampire has become a teen idol and can sell books and DVDs by the million.

The popularity of the Twilight books has led to an abundance of imitators, as a quick scan at the young adult shelves of any bookstore will indicate. Teenaged vampires, usually attractive and brooding, run rampant in young adult fiction.

And the phenomenon is not limited to the young adult market. Vampires star in a broad range of adult fiction—from mysteries to romance to erotic novels. Best-selling authors like Laurell K. Hamilton, Charlaine Harris, Christine Feehan, and Sherrilyn Kenyon have popularized the vampire as a sex object and romantic hero. Adaptations of well-known book series have been hitting the theaters and networks. Vampires have filled our televisions, our movie screens, our bookstores, and our computers in online discussion boards and blogs.

Why has popular culture recently been overrun with vampires, and how are Christians supposed to understand it? Vampires would not have become as popular as they have if they didn't mean something to us as a culture. They represent something to us—something that matters—and that is one of the questions this study seeks to explore. Vampires are more than just monsters to us. They have recurred as a figure in literature and Western culture for the last two centuries, and they go back much further in lore and myth. It is over the last hundred years or so, however, that their portrayal in our culture has morphed from monster to lover, from single-minded villain to complex antihero. The vampire was once held up as the embodiment of evil and temptation, but has now become the ultimate romantic alpha-hero. *The Vampire Defanged* explores how this transformation occurred and what it means to Christians.

Vampire History

To understand how vampires are portrayed today, it helps to know how and where the legend originated. Anthropologists and historians trace vampire lore back to ancient cultures from all over the world. Cultures as far-ranging as Hebrew, Greek, Roman, Indian, Chinese, Egyptian, and pre-Colombian have their own version of myths and stories featuring blood-sucking or life-sucking demons, evil spirits that can animate dead bodies, and bat gods. The characteristics of what the Western world specifically understands as a vampire come primarily from the folklore of southeastern Europe— the Balkan and Slavic cultures specifically. Bram Stoker pulled from a number of different traditions in writing *Dracula*, but focused on the history and culture of Transylvania. Since Dracula has been so central to our understanding of vampires in the Western tradition, the way we understand the vampire is heavily influenced by folklore from that region.

Because of the wide range of cultures with vampire myths, it is difficult to come up with a universal set of vampire characteristics. The two characteristics that seem to be most common, and the two that are usually sustained in contemporary vampire depictions, are these: vampires drink human blood and vampires are animated corpses, not truly alive. Some of the other common additional characteristics that came from southeastern European folklore are the vampire's fear of sunlight, shape-shifting capabilities (often shifting into a wolf or a bat), hypnotic powers, the need to return to their native earth or grave during the day, and death by a wooden stake through the heart. Vampires are also often understood to be afraid of garlic and unable to cross running water.

Once the Catholic Church tradition was integrated into the earlier folklore, the Christian elements were added to the vampire myth, such as aversion to the cross and other holy objects, and the connections between vampires and Satan or his demons. Many scholars speculate that the stories developed in part because of early peoples' inability to understand concepts like decomposition and infection—as well as less common phenomena like premature burial. Burying someone who wasn't truly dead might easily convince people from previous centuries that vampires really exist. So the vampire legend as we understand it today is a mixture of primitive beliefs, European folklore, and Christian influences.

Once the stories were developed in folklore, they began to make an appearance in literature. The vampire appeared in a number of eighteenth-century German poems, and those were the inspiration for the nineteenth-century English literary depictions of vampires, like Polidori's *The Vampyre* (1819), perhaps the first genuine vampire story written in English. Other nineteenth-century vampire stories include *Varney the Vampire*, which was first released in inexpensive pamphlets called the "penny dreadful" in the 1840s and featured one of the first examples of a conflicted vampire. A final nineteenth-century example was Sheridan Le Fanu's *Carmilla* (1872), describing a female vampire. As the vampire myth was first turned into fiction, the associations of the vampire with evil and temptation were established, characteristics that have been diminishing gradually since.

Vampire as Metaphor

While a particular contemporary subculture might believe in literal vampires among us—those individuals who identify themselves as vampires in real life—most people who study or are engaged with vampires do so in a metaphorical sense. We find vampires in our mythology and our fiction, in our film and television. In those contexts, we are attracted to the vampire as metaphor.

Vampires represent something to us as humans. They represent our fears and our desires. The reason they have recurred in our stories over the last hundred years is that vampires are rich enough a metaphor to adapt to culture's changing worldview and interests. We can make a vampire mean what we want it to mean. We can use it for any number of purposes. In her important study of vampires, *Our Vampires, Ourselves*, Nina Auerbach says that "every age embraces the vampire it needs."[1] There is something about the figure of the vampire that attracts us in this metaphorical sense. As a metaphor it hits at the heart of what makes us human. A vampire is a monster that has a human shape, and so it becomes a picture through which we can explore the human condition.

In the last twenty years, scholars and other thinkers have started to study the vampire as a legitimate topic for intellectual inquiry. While some of these studies focus on the cultural origins of the myth itself and some explore the "literal" manifestation of the vampire, other scholars have tried to trace a history of the appearance of the vampire in popular books and media. Usually, this is done by focusing on the vampire as metaphor.[2] Vampires can represent such a variety of concepts for us that it is impossible to make a comprehensive list, but two of the most common in popular culture connect vampires with our fears and our sexual desires or experiences.

Traditionally, the vampire was an evil, frightening figure. Thus, early portraits of vampires tended to represent a culture's fears. In nineteenth-century vampire literature like Coleridge's poem "Christabel" or Le Fanu's *Carmilla*, a vampire was often associated with sexually aggressive females, one of the fears and obsessions of Victorian culture. More recent vampire stories represent more contemporary cultural fears like the AIDS epidemic and the breakdown of the family. Because the vampire is that monster with a mostly human face, a creature that perverts traditional values and feeds on human blood, it becomes a rich representation of what we fear as a culture.

From the beginning of vampire fiction, the figure of the vampire was also associated with sex. We can see this in the early nineteenth-century stories and poems, and the trend continues through contemporary fiction, film, and television. So another kind of metaphor we find in the vampire is that of sexual experience. The vampire act of drinking blood is a fundamentally intimate one, and it involves a certain kind of penetration. It is not surprising that creators of vampire stories have consistently connected the vampire with sexual desire and experience. In early texts, the sexual nature of the vampire act was cast in negative terms. The vampire represented temptation into sin or the forbidden, temptation that attracts us but leads to destruction. More recently, vampires have been eroticized without the morality, and they stand for sex made exciting through a kind of danger. Having sex with someone who wants to drink your blood is obviously dangerous, and many of these stories work because of the (faulty) premise that sex and romance are most exciting when they are dangerous or forbidden. In a lot of popular contemporary vampire novels (those of Meyer, Harris, and Hamilton, for instance), the vampire is as attractive as he is because he represents both the forbidden and the desired.

Vampires can function as metaphors for a number of other concepts as well. Vampires are often associated with nobility, so they can be used to explore social power. (The vampire metaphor can also probe natural and supernatural power.) Family and community is another common metaphor. While vampires in earlier stories were isolated, almost lonely, more recent vampire portraits place them in families or larger communities. All of these metaphors are worth studying as we seek to understand why the vampire is so important to us as a culture. This book will include discussion of most of these to a certain degree but will focus on the vampire as a representation of cultural worldview, particularly as a theological metaphor that helps us to explore themes of sin, redemption, and morality.

Why Should Christians Care about Vampires?

Christians have been slow to embrace the vampire phenomenon. Only within the last couple of years has the first Christian vampire fiction been released, and many Christians find even that rather dubious. Christians often respond to the vampire phenomenon by either trivializing or demonizing it, brushing it aside as insignificant or labeling an entire century of imaginative production as evil and anti-Christian. In these pages I will seek to counter both responses.

On the one hand, vampires are not trivial. If vampires have consistently spoken so strongly to the human condition, then it is important for us to understand them—how and why they are so popular and how they reflect or don't reflect biblical truth. Ignoring a cultural phenomenon as influential as the vampire myth makes it impossible for Christians to learn from it—to reflect on how our culture understands itself, how our worldview has transformed through time, and what it means to be human. Failing to thoughtfully engage with such a phenomenon also leaves Christians open to uncritically accepting the culture around us and thus allowing ourselves to be passively influenced by it.

On the other hand, working from the assumption that any story that features a vampire is evil, demonic, and dangerous is an equally problematic response for Christians, as it is based on a lack of critical thinking and ignores distinctions between how the vampire is portrayed in different contexts. When the vampire is associated with demonic influences, it is usually more deeply connected to the Christian worldview. Often, when the vampire is portrayed without any spiritual associations at all, the message is more subtle but potentially more dangerous for Christians. It is important to explore vampire stories deeply enough to recognize these nuances. God has called Christians to use thoughtful discernment and informed judgment in assessing the world around us, and this study is prompted by that purpose.

Books and films and television programs have power over us, whether we recognize it or not. Only reading and viewing vampire stories well can allow us to engage them constructively. It could be easy for us to naively declare that all vampires are bad, or declare the opposite, like Sookie Stackhouse in *True Blood*: "I don't think Jesus would mind if somebody was a vampire."[3] Unfortunately, the approach a lot of Christians take toward the vampire phenomenon is nearly as uninformed. Even in literary studies, the art of reading well—examining a text closely to discover what it actually says—is being replaced by a focus on sociopolitical agendas. More than anyone else, Christians should know how to read and view well. And we should read the culture around us as deeply and thoughtfully as we read canonical literature. *The Vampire Defanged* offers a close reading of selected vampire stories as a means of better understanding our culture through the lens of the transforming vampire myth.

In *The Vampire Defanged*, I will analyze five central vampire stories, as well as a sampling of others, and use them to trace the transformation of cultural worldview. I do not intend *The Vampire Defanged* to be a complete history of the vampire since *Dracula*, nor do I argue that the five chosen books, films, and television series are the most influential or important portrayals of vampires in cultural history. But they are each good representations of their respective cultural milieu, and they are all of high enough artistic quality to be examined in some depth.

My analysis of Bram Stoker's novel *Dracula* will set the stage for my argument about the vampire. Published in 1897, *Dracula* is an explicitly Christian novel, although modern readers and critics have invariably ignored the novel's religious dimensions. Stoker builds his depiction of the vampire on a foundational Christian worldview, and that worldview shapes the formation of the vampire legend. By using the figure of the vampire as a representation of sin, temptation, and spiritual torment and by identifying the struggle against Dracula as a crusade against evil in the name of Jesus Christ, Stoker uses the vampire for theological reflection and inspires the nature of the vampire legend throughout the following century.

With Anne Rice's *Interview with the Vampire*, the figure of the vampire transformed from its original significance as a representation of sin to its more modern manifestation as a representation of guilt. Throughout the eleven novels of her Vampire Chronicles, Rice's vampires are spiritual creatures who seek to discover their role in a baffling universe. The worldview shaped by her novels progresses through the series—from the existential emptiness of *Interview* to a theology that consistently questions and concludes with no real answers except for the absolute value of love.

Although *Buffy the Vampire Slayer* is a television series that spanned seven seasons and was written and directed by a number of different people, it manages to maintain a unified vision through the work of its creator, Joss Whedon. With the introduction of Angel, the vampire cursed with a soul, haunted by all of his past sins, the series explores theological questions of sin, sacrifice, and redemption with more depth and complexity than most other vampire stories. However, Whedon intentionally divorces the spiritual themes from traditional Christianity and emphasizes elements of paganism that complicate its religious conclusions. Ultimately, the series is a postmodern television program that validates multiple worldviews, even as it affirms the Christian roots of the vampire legend.

My examination of Charlaine Harris's Southern Vampire Mysteries and the HBO series *True Blood*, inspired by the book series, will focus on how the figure of the vampire is secularized in much contemporary vampire fiction. By emphasizing secular manifestations of the vampire figure, focused on sex and social difference, Harris minimizes the spiritual dimensions of traditional vampire characterization. And by compartmentalizing Sookie's Christian worldview and showing its inability to fully encompass a world where the supernatural is reality, the novels present a mostly secular vision of vampires. *True Blood* goes even farther along these lines with a skepticism about the nature of religion as a whole.

Stephenie Meyer's Twilight Saga represents a complete removal of the vampire myth from any sort of Christian or theological significance. By "defanging" her vampires, making them capable of free will and thus little more than glorified humans with a penchant for drinking blood, Meyer strips away the fundamental themes of sin, temptation, and spiritual guilt that have traditionally shaped the vampire myth. In Meyer's novels, the vampire has become completely secularized within an adolescent romantic fantasy.

In the final two chapters of this book, "Vampire Sinners" and "Vampire Saviors," I will pull together a selection of other vampire stories and show how a sampling of vampire tales present a dual portrait of the figure of the vampire. In "Vampire Sinners," I will examine how the traditional emphasis on sin in the nature of the vampire is transformed in different ways—minimized in service of a suspenseful mood, humanized by the creation of half-vampire characters, and shaped into a picture of amoral vampire community. In "Vampire Saviors," I will focus on how vampires have become domesticated or become heroes in many contemporary stories. This happens by turning them into tortured but repentant do-gooders, romantic partners for humans, or sex objects—and also by focusing on power rather than moral issues.

Vampires matter to us—as individuals and as a culture. By closely attending to their representations, we can better understand why they are important to us and what we can learn from them.

2

Bram Stoker's *Dracula*

Sin and the Power of the Cross

Thus we are ministers of God's own wish: that the world, and men for whom His Son die, will not be given over to monsters, whose very existence would defame Him.

Van Helsing in Stoker's *Dracula*

In the first chapter of Bram Stoker's novel *Dracula*, a Transylvanian peasant woman gives Jonathan Harker her own crucifix, after pleading with him not to keep traveling to the malevolent Castle Dracula. Harker, a self-proclaimed English churchman (and so someone deeply opposed to Roman Catholicism), hesitates to take something he has been taught to consider "in some measure idolatrous."[1] He accepts the crucifix out of courtesy and is infinitely grateful for it later, after he meets the castle's diabolical master. The crucifix saves his life. In *Dracula*, the power of the Christian cross is more than simply a plot device. The cross is a picture of one of the central themes of the novel, and it points to the way Stoker portrays the figure of the vampire. The vampire in *Dracula* is used for spiritual and theological reflection in a way that is gradually secularized as the vampire genre develops through the twentieth century.

The symbol of the cross has become so commonplace in vampire mythology that many readers overlook its significance in *Dracula*, lumping the symbol in with the creepy castle and the howling of wolves as features of the Gothic genre intended to build suspense or create a supernatural ambience.[2] Stoker uses the cross in a far more significant way, however, and we must take the symbol seriously if we are to read the novel well. The image of a vampire cringing from the sight of a crucifix or hissing in pain from direct contact with a rosary has been used so often in the last century that it has become almost clichéd. As we will explore later, the most recent vampire stories have eliminated the vampire's traditional fear of sacred objects entirely, perhaps in an attempt to craft something new out of the genre. But *Dracula*, while certainly not the first vampire novel, and itself drawing on a long tradition of vampire lore,[3] is the novel that set the stage for images and plot devices that have since become clichés. And Stoker makes it clear that the symbol of the cross should highlight the novel's spiritual themes and purpose.

None of the religious symbols or theological themes of *Dracula* is handled simplistically, nor is Christianity accepted as foundational by rote or without consideration. In fact, the principal characters' skeptical views call the reality of religious and supernatural power into question throughout the novel. Early on, after Harker has spent a few days in Castle Dracula, and after he has realized that he is a prisoner there, he reflects on the rosary the Transylvanian peasant has given him:

> Bless that good, good woman who hung the crucifix round my neck! For it is a comfort and a strength to me whenever I touch it. It is odd that a thing which I have been taught to regard with disfavor and as idolatrous should in a time of loneliness and trouble be of help. Is it that there is something in the essence of the thing itself, or that it is a medium, a tangible help, in conveying memories of sympathy and comfort? Some time, if it may be, I must examine this matter and try to make up my mind about it.[4]

Harker doesn't immediately understand the significance of the gift he has been given, even after he has seen Dracula recoil from contact with the crucifix. He tries to explain it away as simply a tangible sign of kindness in the midst of trouble. But the unfolding events of the novel reveal the cross's true theological significance.

What, then, does the symbol of the cross have to do with the novel's portrayal of the vampire? The cross and the figure of the vampire in *Dracula* are inextricably linked. Once the cross has been understood theologically in the context of the novel, then the vampire must be as well. The vampire—primarily Count Dracula himself—represents all of the forces that the cross must defeat. It is easy to say that the vampire is a representation of evil. It may be true, but it is overly simplistic and, until the last few decades, was almost universally true of the many manifestations of vampires in literary and popular culture. The figure of the vampire in *Dracula* is more complex than a force of generic evil. Because the evil is placed in a spiritual context, the vampire comes to represent sin in a theological sense. With the portrayal of sin in the figure of the vampire, Stoker also tackles related themes of temptation, blood, spiritual torment, and the Christian as spiritual warrior. Although these religious aspects of the novel are often overlooked in contemporary readings, they are fundamental to understanding how Stoker develops his story.[5]

In the following analysis of *Dracula*, I will examine some of these religious elements. First, I will argue for the connections between the vampire and sin in *Dracula*. These connections are affirmed by Stoker's emphasis on the spiritual threat the vampire poses for humans, a threat even more dangerous than the physical. Then, an analysis of Stoker's use of the religious symbols of the narrative sets the stage for understanding how the characters become Christian warriors in a spiritual battle. And, finally, we will see that salvation in *Dracula*—salvation *from* Dracula—ultimately comes only through faith.

The Fangs of Sin

The first section of *Dracula* is made up of Jonathan Harker's experiences in Castle Dracula as the Count's prisoner. As is typical for Gothic novels, Stoker employs a number of narrative strategies, perspectives, and narrators, primarily using letters and journals to tell the story. Harker's experiences after arriving to act as Dracula's solicitor are shared through his journal-style letters to his fiancée, Mina, and through them readers are given their first picture of the vampire as the embodiment of sin. While it is not difficult to see how Dracula represents evil—after all, he lies to, imprisons, and psychologically tortures Harker and then leaves him to die, all within the first few chapters of the novel—the assumption that the vampire is a picture of sin requires more examination.

The first image Harker has of Dracula comes before he or the reader recognizes the man's identity. The figure acting as coachman on the last leg of Harker's journey is described as tall with a brown beard and a big black hat. Only his reddish eyes and "sharp-looking teeth" hint at his true nature.[6] When Harker arrives at the castle, he meets the man again as Count Dracula, this time described as having a long white mustache and being clad entirely in black. The further physical descriptions we receive of Dracula over the next chapters include a hand "as cold as ice—more like the hand of a dead than a living man," a strong nose with arched nostrils, a high forehead, bushy eyebrows, a "cruel-looking" mouth with unnaturally red lips, oddly pointed ears, and hands with hair growing on the palms.[7]

Although Dracula in Stoker's novel doesn't look like movie actor Bela Lugosi, most commonly envisioned by contemporary audiences, the thematic significance of his physical appearance should be apparent. Unlike contemporary pictures of the vampire from novels like Anne Rice's and Stephenie Meyer's, the vampire here is not beautiful. The vampire is connected with death in his coldness and pallor and connected to predators with his sharp teeth and the heightened sense of smell implied by his arched nostrils. The pointed ears perhaps imply demonic roots, along with the hair on the palms. But primarily it is the unnaturalness of his appearance that seems at issue—in multiple ways, Dracula is embodied as not quite human. Certainly he is not something humans should be or would want to be. This impression is affirmed later when Harker sees him crawl across the castle wall like a reptile. After Rice's *Interview with the Vampire*, the figure of the vampire in contemporary culture became more and more humanized—and now it is often idealized, like Edward in *Twilight*, who Bella consistently compares to an angel. But not so in *Dracula*. Dracula's physical appearance points toward the vampire's significance as a representation of sin. But, more than simply his appearance, his behavior with Harker sets up the emphasis on sin which is further developed in the remainder of the novel.

One noteworthy feature of Count Dracula is the way his speech pattern faintly mirrors biblical language. In the first evening's conversation, Dracula uses Moses's language of being a "stranger in a strange land."[8] Later, he says that if Harker could "see with my eyes and know with my knowledge, you would perhaps better understand,"[9] a phrase that seems to mirror Isaiah 6:10—". . . lest they see with their eyes, and hear with their ears, and understand with their heart, and convert, and be healed." Dracula also says in the next paragraph, "Our ways are not your ways"[10]—a less obvious reference to another passage in Isaiah 55:8: "For my thoughts are not your thoughts, neither are your ways my ways, saith the LORD." The biblical references continue in Dracula's speech pattern. While it might be a stretch to argue for too much meaning in the details of these references, they certainly open up Dracula's character to potential spiritual significance.

Perhaps the clearest argument for Dracula's connection to sin in a theological sense, however, can be seen in the way the first four chapters (Harker's experiences in Castle Dracula) allow the figure of the vampire to display each of the seven deadly sins. Some of these sins are obvious. Dracula displays *wrath*, for instance, a number of times—his face reflecting a "demoniac fury" when Harker cuts himself with a razor[11] or bursting into rage like the "demons of the pit" when he catches the three female vampires about to feed on Harker.[12]

Gluttony too is not difficult to find—the vampire's unnatural desire to feed on blood has always been its primary characteristic and is certainly true of both Dracula and the female vampires, the "weird sisters," with whom he shares his castle. One of the most startling images in the early part of the novel is when Harker finds Dracula resting unconscious in his box after having fed on a victim:

> There lay the Count, but looking as if his youth had been half renewed, for the white hair and moustache were changed to dark iron-grey; the cheeks were fuller and the white skin seemed ruby-red underneath; the mouth was redder than ever, for on the lips were gouts of fresh blood, which trickled from the corners of the mouth and ran over the chin and the neck. Even the deep, burning eyes seemed set amongst swollen flesh, for the lids and pouches underneath were bloated. It seemed as if the whole awful creature were simply gorged with blood; he lay like a filthy leech exhausted with his repletion.[13]

The grotesque image is a graphic picture of gluttony in its most unnatural and revolting state.

In addition to wrath and gluttony, however, we see *lust*, *envy*, and *greed* associated with the figure of the vampire. When Harker stumbles on the weird sisters after the sun has set, their assault on him is clearly described in sexual terms. They are described as beautiful and mesmerizing with "voluptuous lips" and similar characteristics such as "masses of golden hair." Harker feels in his heart "a wicked, burning desire that they would kiss [him] with those red lips." Harker waits in "delightful anticipation" for them to feed on him, and the resulting sensations are described in sensual terms— "honey sweet," "deliberate voluptuousness," "tingle," "languorous ecstasy."[14] Without doubt, lust is associated with the nature of the vampire, and this eroticism is sustained throughout most vampire portraits that follow. Immediately following this scene, Dracula enters in his most violent rage. He hisses at the sisters, "How dare you touch him, any of you? How dare you cast eyes on him when I had forbidden it? Back, I tell you all! This man belongs to me!"[15] Thus, envy becomes a feature of vampire behavior, as the female vampires desire what Dracula possesses. Greed or avarice makes an appearance too, as Harker finds a huge pile of gold in one of the rooms of Castle Dracula, a traditional image for avarice.

The final two of the deadly sins are usually listed as *pride* and *sloth*. Dracula shows pride on more than one occasion in boasting the nobility of his heritage—even saying at one point his family has "a right to be proud."[16] Sloth is more difficult to find in the book. In fact, unless one argues that the vampire's necessary "sleep" in the boxes of earth is an example of sloth, the sin is not evident in the first section of the novel. However, in the church's earlier lists of deadly sins the sin was *acedia*—despair—which later transformed into sloth. We can certainly see despair as a prominent feature of Stoker's portrayal of the vampire. In one of their early conversations, Dracula tells Harker:

> We Transylvanian nobles love not to think that our bones may be amongst the common dead. I see not gaiety nor mirth, not the bright voluptuousness of much sunshine and sparkling waters which please the young and gay. I am no longer young; and my heart, through weary years of mourning over the dead, is not attuned to mirth. Moreover, the walls of my castle are broken; the shadows are many, and the wind breathes cold through the broken battlements and casements. I love the shade and the shadow, and would be alone with my thoughts when I may.[17]

Dracula is defined by the shadows of despair as much as by his wrath and his desire to feed.

So each of the seven deadly sins can be seen in the portrayal of the vampire in the first four chapters of the novel. It is hard to ignore how closely Stoker aligns the person of the vampire with a theological understanding of sin. During his experiences at the castle, Harker is tantalized by the allure of sin, hypnotized into failing to fight against it, victimized and imprisoned by it, and finally threatened to death by it. Ultimately, Harker, who began the journey with a secular perspective that explained away the religious power of the cross, understands the threat he faces as not only supernatural but also theological. Before he makes his last attempt to escape, he claims the castle is a "cursed land, where the devil and his children still walk with earthly feet."[18] He looks to God's mercy at the end of his last letter, but it is not until later in the novel that we see how God's mercy to those humans threatened by the vampire—certainly by evil but more specifically by sin—can be found.

To Hell and Back: Sin's Victim

While nearly all of the characters are affected by the power of the vampires in the novel, Lucy Westenra functions as a graphic example of a character who suffers the whole cycle of victimization. A close examination of Lucy's character can help us see more clearly how the novel uses the figure of the vampire to reflect on theological questions.

Readers grow to know Lucy Westenra through the letters between her and Mina and through the diaries that Mina and later Lucy herself writes. While Lucy is never a fully developed character, we can recognize a few important features of her nature through the contrast between her and Mina. Both women are young, apparently innocent, sweet-natured, and inexperienced. Both seem to have a genuine affection for each other. But, as many critics have pointed out, Lucy is more of a sexual object than is Mina. Her second letter in the novel is an announcement of having received three marriage proposals in one day, and shortly after this announcement she asks the somewhat scandalous question, "Why can't they let a girl marry three [men], or as many as want her, and save all this trouble?"[19] While she immediately takes back the question as heresy, it does point toward a less demure and traditional character than we see in Mina.

A common reading of the novel takes clues of this kind and argues that Lucy is punished for her unrestrained sexual nature, as Stoker sets up proper Victorian chastity as the only appropriate role for women. This reading is a good one—for Stoker does sexualize the figure of the vampire and a number of aspects of Lucy's descent into vampirism.[20] But to limit the contrast between Lucy and Mina to merely one of their sexuality is to ignore all of the theological implications of Stoker's characterization.

Another significant difference between the characters can be seen in the way that Lucy's character is always more self-oriented than Mina's. While Mina's concerns are almost exclusively for other people—for her fiancée, Harker, for Lucy, for Mrs. Westenra—Lucy spends much of her time talking and thinking about herself. She is disturbed by the way she has to hurt her two rejected suitors and she certainly has no malicious or callous intentions, but her focus is almost entirely on her own experiences, feelings, concerns, and desires—a sharp contrast with Mina. This distinction is important as it opens Lucy up to Dracula's assault. He chooses her before he does Mina, perhaps because she is an easier victim, already prone to fall under the spell of men and less focused on loftier virtues.

Dracula's assault on her is a physical one, of course, but it is also a spiritual one. As Lucy falls more and more under his power, her will as much as her body is affected. In fact, Dracula begins his influence on her mentally and spiritually, with some kind of hypnosis that occurs without actual physical contact. Lucy begins to become restless and starts to sleepwalk as she falls under his power. The actual encounter when Dracula claims her is sexualized, to be sure—she is a small, unclad, white figure beneath a large, dark figure crouching over her—but it is also spiritualized. When Lucy describes the assault to Mina afterward (neither yet realizing it was an assault), Lucy says:

> Then I had a vague memory of something long and dark with red eyes, just as we saw in the sunset, and something very sweet and very bitter all around me at once. And then I seemed sinking into deep green water, and there was a singing in my ears, as I have heard there is to drowning men, and then everything seemed passing away from me; my soul seemed to go out from my body and float about the air. I seem to remember that once the West Lighthouse was right under me, and then there was a sort of agonizing feeling, as if I were in an earthquake, and I came back and found you shaking my body. I saw you do it before I felt you.[21]

The spiritual here is just as important as the physical—her soul's leaving her body is the most distinct memory she has of the experience. And, following Dracula's claiming of her, she shifts back and forth between illness and evident health, but she also shifts between emotional poles of cheerfulness and languid despair. While Lucy never understands herself theologically or religiously, the real battle that is waged is for her soul rather than for her body. In fact, the physical manifestations of the assault, often posed in sexual terms, seem to be in service of the spiritual rather than the other way around.[22]

The spiritual nature of her transformation into a vampire is made evident, of course, after she becomes "Un-Dead" and starts to assault children as the "Bloofer Lady." The religious icons are the tools that can hold her at bay—the crucifix and, more powerfully, the Host. Later in this chapter, I will explore the significance of the religious objects used against the vampires, but for now what is important is that the fight for Lucy's salvation is a spiritual battle. When others see her in her form as Un-Dead, her internal transformation has been manifested in her physical appearance: "She seemed like a nightmare of Lucy as she lay there; the pointed teeth, the bloodstained, voluptuous mouth—which it made one shudder to see—the whole carnal and unspiritual appearance, seeing like a devilish mockery of Lucy's sweet purity." The only option is to kill her for real and thus free her soul for heaven. As Van Helsing explains, in her vampire form she is cursed to multiply evil in the world, but being freed she can "take her place with the other Angels."

Through prayer and a stake through the heart in God's name, they are able to save her from the curse of being a vampire. And, once it is over, her body reflects a "holy calm" that is an "earthly token and symbol" of her salvation.[23] It is no coincidence that the bodily form reflects the spiritual reality—both in her descent into evil and her recovery from it. While it would be simplifying the novel to claim that vampirism is only a symbol or representation of something else—sin, evil, and so on—it is certainly overlooking one of Stoker's main purposes to ignore the spiritual significance of the figure of the vampire as it is portrayed in the novel. Because Stoker uses the person of the vampire for theological reflection, all of the action around it takes on spiritual resonance.

Religious Symbols: Blood and the Tools of Christian Warfare

In chapter 11 of *Dracula*, the asylum patient Renfield invades Dr. Seward's study and cuts the doctor with a dinner knife.

As the attendants rush in and carry the patient away, Renfield repeats over and over again, "The blood is the life! The blood is the life!"[24] Any good student of the Bible will recognize this statement from Deuteronomy 12:23, where God directs his people not to eat blood because it is the life of a being. Renfield repeats the phrase later in the novel, in one of his bouts of sanity, as he attempts to explain his behavior. Under Dracula's indirect hypnotic influence, Renfield has felt compelled to strengthen his own life powers by partaking of the blood of someone else.

Every week in the sacrament of the Eucharist, the Lord's Supper, Christians symbolically eat of Christ's body and drink of his blood as a sign and a seal of their union with him. It is not a great leap of deduction to recognize the vampire's drinking of human blood as an inversion of this act of Christian devotion. In the Christian worldview, eternal life only comes through Christ—through his spilt blood on the cross in defeat of sin and through his resurrection. Vampires, however, find a different kind of eternal life in digesting human blood. As Van Helsing explains, "When they become such, there comes with the change the curse of immortality; they cannot die, but must go on age after age adding new victims and multiplying the evils of the world."[25]

In *Dracula*, unlike in later vampire stories, this eternal life is purposefully opposed to the eternal life found in Christ. We can see this in the way Lucy must be "killed" again in order for her soul to be free for heaven. Renfield, in his conversation with Dr. Seward, also drives home this opposition. He makes a distinction between desiring "life" by eating other life forms and wanting "souls." "Oh no, oh no!" he says, "I want no souls. Life is all I want." Then he says about God, "I am not even concerned in His especially spiritual doings."[26] Not only is the vampire urge in opposition to Christian salvation,

25

it is posed as a demonic inversion of it. When Dracula approaches Renfield to tempt him into doing his will, Renfield understands him to be saying, "All these lives will I give you, ay, and many more and great through countless ages, if you will fall down and worship me"—words obviously echoing Satan's temptation of Christ in the Gospels.[27]

It is by Christ's blood that the Christian is saved. And, in *Dracula*, the unnatural drinking of blood in an inversion of Holy Communion is a means of human damnation. When Lucy suffers physically from the loss of blood, Van Helsing knows that she needs a transfusion of blood to keep her alive. But this doesn't, of course, get to the root of the problem—a spiritual one, not a physical one—so the medical treatment only works temporarily. A religious ceremony is necessary. Spiritual warfare is the only way to save in the face of a spiritual threat.

Like the drinking of blood, the Christian iconography has become such a standard part of vampire lore that its significance is often overlooked in *Dracula*. But in Stoker's novel, Christian images are used for thematic purposes as well as being devices of the plot. In chapter 18, as a kind of rallying speech to inspire the collection of devoted participants in the struggle against Dracula, Van Helsing puts into words the Christian mission of the battle:

> My friends, this is much; it is a terrible task that we undertake, and there may be consequences to make the brave shudder. For if we fail in this our fight he must surely win: and then where end we? Life is nothings; I heed him not. But to fail here, is not mere life or death. It is that we become as him; that we henceforward become foul things of the night like him—without heart or conscience, preying on the bodies and the souls of those we love best. To us for ever are the gates of heaven shut; for who shall open them to us again?

We go on for all time abhorred by all; a blot on the face of God's sunshine; an arrow in the side of Him who died for man. But we are face to face with duty; and in such case must we shrink?"[28]

Again, we cannot read the novel as a simple allegory, drawing a clear, Christian, one-to-one correspondence for its readers. The fight against the vampires doesn't cleanly translate into the struggle of Christians against sin or evil in the world. But it reflects Christian truths using the rules of the fictional world. That is, eternal matters are of more significance than worldly matters (notice how Van Helsing makes it clear that what they are doing is more important than life or death). Sin and evil cannot be tolerated, as it is an affront to God's nature. Thus Christians have a responsibility to resist it, knowing they can only do so through the power of God.

In the novel, the power of God is illustrated through the use of Christian symbols. Repeatedly, the vampire in the novel is helpless when confronted with the crucifix. And, being a good Christian, Van Helsing gets a private indulgence from the Vatican to use the Host in his war against the vampires.[29] A lot of modern readers lump these religious symbols in with the other supernatural elements used in the plot that come from pagan or non-Christian traditions—the garlic, for instance, that is also used by Van Helsing against the vampires. Certainly, Stoker pulls from various traditions in creating his vampire mythology, but even the pagan objects are used in the context of a Christian mission to fight the evil of the vampire.

More importantly, the Christian objects are always given a privileged place in the story. We can see this most graphically as the novel builds to its climax and the small band of Christians fights to save Mina from Dracula. After she has encountered Dracula, Mina cringes back from the crucifix around her husband's neck and calls herself "Unclean, unclean" (as the Mosaic Law directs the leper in Leviticus 13:45).[30] And when Van Helsing blesses Mina for protection, placing the wafer of the Host against her forehead in the name of God, it literally burns into her skin, causing her to cry out once more, "Unclean, unclean."[31] It is the Christian objects that have the most power in this fight in a novel that is ultimately a Christian one.

When Mina despairs that her flesh is contaminated, violated by Dracula, and no longer pleasing to God, Van Helsing encourages her, voicing the ultimate truth of Stoker's Christian message:

> For so surely as we live, that scar shall pass away when God sees right to lift the burden that is hard upon us. Till then we bear our Cross, as his Son did in obedience to His will. It may be that we are chosen instruments of His good pleasure, and that we ascend to His bidding as that other through stripes and shame, through tears and blood; through doubts and fears, and all that makes the difference between God and man.[32]

Later he reaffirms this mission by labeling their purposes as a Christian crusade: "Thus we are ministers of God's own wish: that the world, and men for whom His Son die, will not be given over to monsters, whose very existence would defame Him."[33]

In *Dracula*, theological ideas are consistently given tangible form—evil is embodied in the vampire, the curse of sin embodied in the mark on Mina's head—so it is not surprising that the power of God in the fight against darkness is embodied in Christian symbols like the crucifix and the Host. While Harker, at the beginning of the novel, with his enlightened skepticism, wonders what makes the crucifix such a powerful comfort to him, it is clear by the end that it is not some sort of vague supernatural power in the essence of the object or the comfort of an emotional attachment to the symbol. Rather it is the power of God through traditional representations of God's work in the world.

Salvation through Faith

One of the common readings of *Dracula* juxtaposes the worldview of scientific reason with the superstition of the past. Without doubt, this is a thread that runs through the novel. From the beginning, Harker prides himself on his reason and skepticism, only to be confronted with the reality of the local superstitions in the terrible person of Dracula. Dr. Seward, a scientist, relies on the scientific method in his observations of Renfield, only to come to the conclusion that science can only get him so far in discovering the truth of Renfield's malady. Van Helsing himself has a worldview based on a combination of science—he is a doctor, after all, and uses methods like medical blood transfusions in his attempt to combat Dracula's influence—and faith. He knows, more than any other character in the novel, that there are "mysteries in life" that modern reason and science simply cannot answer.[34] The vampire is one of these mysteries, and Dracula has as much power as he does in large part because the modern world simply cannot believe in him.

The first step in fighting him, then, is faith. Again, Van Helsing is the spokesperson of Stoker's themes. He explains to Dr. Seward as a way of gradually leading him to the truth about what happened to Lucy:

"My thesis is this: I want you to believe."
"To believe in what?"

> "To believe in things that you cannot. Let me illustrate. I heard once of an American who so defined faith: 'that which enables us to believe things which we know to be untrue.' For one, I follow that man. He meant that we shall have an open mind, and not let a little bit of truth check the rush of a big truth, like a small rock does a railway truck. We get the small truth first. Good! We keep him, and we value him; but all the same we must not let him think himself all the truth in the universe."[35]

It takes faith to begin to fight against the forces of evil. Certainly, part of faith here is associated with superstition, and Stoker doesn't always distinguish between religious faith and a general faith in things we don't understand. But, more and more as the plot develops, "faith" becomes clearly connected with religion, and the faith that ultimately saves is a faith in God's power.

The best example of the saving power of faith and the most powerful illustration of Stoker's handling of theology can be seen in Mina's story. The process of Dracula's influence over her initially mirrors that of Lucy's. But Mina has more virtues to draw on than Lucy, and she has more support in fighting against Dracula in the circle of men who surrounded her, armed with the knowledge Van Helsing provides. As I mentioned before, Dracula's claiming of her leads to a "pollution" of her body. In some ways, her body is turned over to his power as Lucy's was before. Although they are all aware of it, there is no way to completely stop Dracula's hypnotic influence over her. And all know that, unless something intervenes, eventually she will be under his power completely and become a vampire like him.

Van Helsing, however, turns the situation over to God, and the other characters seem to recognize this necessity as well. As Harker says in his journal, reflecting on Mina's situation,

"My only comfort is that we are in the hands of God. Only for that faith it would be easier to die than to live, and so be quit of all the trouble."[36] Later Mina says the same thing, "We are truly in the hands of God."[37] Only through God's grace can Mina be saved from the evil that has infected her body, visibly embodied in the scar from the Host on her forehead. The biblical connections here are obvious—the mark of Cain, the Passover ritual which was to be like a "symbol on your forehead" of what God had done for the Israelites (Exodus 13:16 NIV), and the mark on the forehead in the book of Revelation, associated with either God or the Beast. Biblically, a mark on the forehead signifies an individual's identity and is a constant, visible reminder of that identity. Thus Mina is contaminated with evil, with sin, and the burning mark of the Host proves that to the world until she is made clean again.

It takes faith for all of them to pursue Dracula across Europe until they can find him sleeping and kill him. Quincey Morris actually dies in the attempt, but his sacrifice, like the sacrifice of the rest of them in doing their duty and fulfilling God's will, is worth it because of the reward:

> The sun was now right down upon the mountain top, and the red gleams fell upon my [Mina's] face, so that it was bathed in rosy light. With one impulse the men sank on their knees and a deep and earnest "Amen" broke from all as their eyes following the pointing of his finger as the dying man spoke:—
>
> "Now God be thanked that all has not been in vain! See! the snow is not more stainless than her forehead! The curse has passed away!"[38]

Mina is cleansed of Dracula's power, the evil contaminating her body, and the signifying mark on her forehead disappears as soon as Dracula is killed. Her guilt is washed clean. And that is only accomplished by a group of Christians doing their

31

best, through sacrifice, to do the duty God has called them to. It is through faith that the victory comes. Certainly, readers are not wrong when they notice that Stoker is valuing faith in mysteries of all kinds as opposed to the limits of scientific reason. But he is also pointing toward a very particular kind of religious faith—faith that God's will is good and the duty of each Christian is to follow God's will, no matter what the consequences.

Any thoughtful reader of *Dracula* will realize that Stoker is calling on Christian beliefs and tradition to develop his portrayal of the vampire and to empower the characters who must fight against it. But critical consensus has implied the Christian elements are peripheral to the heart of the novel or else an artificial imposition on what would otherwise have been a compelling read.[39] The Christian worldview is fundamental to *Dracula*, however, and it therefore lays the foundation for the future of the vampire in literary and popular stories to follow. Stoker uses the vampire to reflect on theological questions about sin and salvation. As we move through stories that come after *Dracula*, we will see how these spiritual issues are minimized and then transformed into something secular as the vampire genre adapts to a shifting cultural worldview. As Christian theology is lost in the characterization, the vampire loses his fangs.

3

Anne Rice's Vampire Chronicles

Eternal Guilt and Transcendent Love

We have souls, you and I. We want to know things; we share the same earth, rich and verdant and fraught with perils.

Lestat in *Memnoch the Devil*

In *Conversations with Anne Rice*, by Michael Riley, Anne Rice reflects on one of the underlying themes in the early Vampire Chronicles. She says, "Obviously there's a great effort in the books to go back and reclaim and acknowledge the tremendous power of all that history of the Church and to search for another truth in it, a truth other than that which it presents to the world, which I felt had to be rejected."[1] This attempt to "redeem" Christian thought and history is evident in all eleven novels of Rice's Vampire Chronicles, although the means through which she does so transforms in each novel. Later in *Conversations*, Riley asks her directly if she believes

33

in God, and she answers that she does but she doesn't "know exactly what that belief means."[2] Rice's comments here help to set the stage for an examination of her spiritual and theological explorations through her portrait of the vampire.

Although she was raised a Catholic, Anne Rice rejected the Christian faith as a student and sustained that rejection for much of her career. In 1998, however, Rice returned to the church. In 2002 she committed her writing to Christ, her conversion widely publicized and evidenced by a new series of novels on the life of Christ. In July 2010 she publicly announced on her Facebook page that she had "quit being a Christian" in the "name of Christ," but she consistently distinguished between her rejection of organized religion and her personal love for Christ.[3] Her vampire fiction is not Christian, and the Vampire Chronicles sometimes explore ideas that are theologically controversial. But the assumption—made by many Christians—that her early novels are immoral or even demonic does not hold up under a close reading. In fact, the novels give evidence of the spiritual transformation in Rice's own life. By closely examining the portrayal of the vampire in the Vampire Chronicles, we can see a working out of Rice's personal theological questions and reflections about Christ.

Rice's vampires are not the simple demonic force that we saw in *Dracula*. They are self-reflective, capable of guilt, and focused on their own consciousness. More than that, they are spiritual beings. They are often, in fact, connected to angels in their appearance (their glowing skin and eyes), in the response they provoke in others, and in their lofty spirituality. They are not afraid of the cross or other sacred objects like holy water or the Host,[4] unless they are absorbed in a cultural system of beliefs that causes them to be so, because they are not the pure demon of vampire tradition. Rice uses the vampire to explore spiritual issues, and those issues become more theological as the Vampire Chronicles progress.

Most readers and scholars agree that Rice's *Interview with the Vampire* was a turning point in the tradition of vampire mythology and literature because of the way Rice abruptly shifted the narrative perspective from the vampire hunters to the vampires themselves and gave her vampires a complex consciousness.[5] Rice also marks a shift in the Christian worldview of the vampire tradition. She continues the tradition set up in *Dracula* that uses the vampire as a catalyst for spiritual reflection. Like Stoker, she connects the vampire to issues of sin, guilt, and the fight against evil, and she uses Christian symbolism, as well as the more universal symbol of blood, to develop the themes. She adds to that theological exploration the theme of redemption, something Stoker himself never really tackles. Unlike in *Dracula*, however, Rice's theological conclusions are not consistently Christian. She embraces some Christian doctrines while adding elements of other forms of spirituality, including paganism and a nihilistic philosophy. Her vampires are not secularized—spirituality is always at issue with them—but her novels reveal a significant step in the progression toward secularizing the figure of the vampire by removing them from a universe shaped by a consistent Christian worldview and by emphasizing the carnal.[6]

Life in Death: An Existence of Eternal Guilt

Anne Rice begins her Vampire Chronicles with 1976's *Interview with the Vampire*. The mood and thematic conclusions of this book are somewhat different from the novels that follow in the series, and most readers can see evidence of Rice's own admission that the novel was a way of working through her grief at the death of her five-year-old daughter a few years earlier.[7] The narrative of *Interview* is overwhelmed with despair and is climaxed by the death of a deathless child. In the novel, very little of the explicit Christian reflection we find in her later novels is evident, but she does establish her interest in church ceremony and mystery as an imaginative motif.[8] She also establishes a foundational theme for the entire series: guilt. The vampire for Anne Rice is not a representation of sin and sin's consequences—rather, the vampire provides a picture of guilt. Rice's most important vampire characters are inevitably plagued by guilt in one form or another.

This theme of guilt is established in *Interview* with Louis, the vampire prompted to tell his story to a newspaper reporter—referred to in the book only as "the Boy." The story Louis tells is part confession, part lesson, and part explanation of his nature and existence. We immediately see a distinction from Stoker in the way that Rice's vampires are beautiful rather than monstrous like Dracula. They are far more humanized in nature than Dracula, and that humanness takes visual form in Louis's physical appearance—he is like a man but paler and more beautiful. He is also humanized by his tendency to feel guilty. Guilt is set up as dominant in his character from the very beginning, as he explains the death of his brother, the central event of his human life and the experience that led him to become vulnerable to a vampire attack in the first place.

Louis's brother was religious. Louis says, "Prayer was what mattered to him, prayer and his leather-bound lives of the saints."[9] When his brother claimed to have religious visions and Louis refused to believe in them, the resulting argument led to his brother's accidental death. Louis's guilt is therefore religiously oriented, and it leads to a despair that makes him wish for death. It is worth noting that Neil Jordan's film version of *Interview with the Vampire* changes the nature of Louis's early despair. Instead of guilt over the death of a brother, Louis (Brad Pitt) in the film is consumed by grief over the death of his wife and child. While that backstory certainly fits many of the themes of the book and creates a nice parallel for Claudia's death in the end, it removes the guilt from the religious context it is given in the novel. Lestat finds Louis in this state of guilt, with the desire to be "thoroughly damned,"[10] attacks him, and then transforms him into a vampire. Thus from the very beginning, the vampire is defined by guilt.

Guilt leads Louis, as he goes through the story of his life and experiences, to express a very clear spiritual struggle between the needs and desires of his vampire nature and his shame over the actions his nature leads him to. A vampire, at least in Anne Rice's mythology, must kill to feed. And Louis, after a confused introduction to vampire existence, resorts to drinking animal blood because he cannot stand the guilt of taking human life. However, his nature always urges him to murder, despite his attempts to control it—and that is one of the central struggles in the novel. At various points, he desperately tries to understand his nature and spiritual condition. His most primal urge is for human blood—an urge, which when satisfied, he enjoys with erotic pleasure—but this urge also leads him to be a killer. He asks, "Am I damned? Am I from the devil? Is my very nature that of the devil?"[11] Louis constantly questions his vampire nature in traditional moral terms, but he never reaches any traditional moral answers.

Later, in encountering a priest in St. Louis Cathedral after he and Claudia together destroy Lestat, Louis says, "Bless me, father, for I have sinned, sinned so often and so long I do not know how to change, nor how to confess before God what I've done."[12] His attempt to confess his nature and his sins fails, as the priest does not believe his

37

claim to be a vampire. The universal nature of his despair and confusion is evidenced in his desperate question to the priest, "Why, if God exists, does He suffer me to exist!"[13] The irony of his situation is made clear when he ends the confession by attacking the priest from whom he is seeking absolution—thus confirming his nature (at least to himself) as sinful. He feels like he belongs to the devil, and at one point he admits that it would actually be a "consolation" to know that Satan exists and that Louis belonged to him completely.[14] He never gets that consolation, however. The nihilistic perspective of the novel prevents an affirmation of even such a dark truth.

Louis's despair and guilt in *Interview* lead him on a kind of quest—a search for meaning and for answers about the existence of God, the devil, and the nature of the vampire in this theological context.[15] His quest leads him with Claudia into Europe, on a search for other vampires who might be able to provide answers to these questions. Louis finally finds a kind of answer in Paris, when they encounter Armand and the other vampires of the *Theatre de Vampire*. But the answers Louis is left with are hardly satisfying. Louis questions Armand, "Then God does not exist . . . you have no knowledge of His existence?" And Armand answers, "None." When Louis follows up with, "And no vampire here has discourse with God or with the devil!" Armand answers, "No vampire that I've ever known."[16] This lack of answer, this lack of knowledge or certainty of God's existence or a universe that has purpose and makes sense is at the heart of Louis's despair. He feels endlessly guilty because of his vampire nature, but there is no answer for that guilt because the world does not provide clear meaning and purpose.

The only conclusions the novel offers affirm the condition of existential angst—a state of universal uncertainty that disallows the possibility of happiness or contentment. When Armand calls Louis the "spirit" of his age, Louis objects to the categorization:

> "No, no." I threw up my hands. I was on the point of a bitter, hysterical laughter. "Don't you see? I'm not the spirit of any age. I'm at odds with everything and always have been! I have never belonged anywhere with anyone at any time!" It was too painful, too perfectly true.[17]

The irony, of course, as Armand explains, is that Louis's state of perpetual unease—verging on nihilism—*is* the spirit of his age. It is a universal condition.[18]

At the end of the novel, Louis explains his state of being with even more clarity. The death of Claudia is an experience that he cannot get over. He can't seem to come "back to life" after it occurs. And he defines the only spiritual experience the novel validates:

> "I wanted love and goodness in this which is living death," I said. "It was impossible from the beginning, because you cannot have love and goodness when you do what you know to be evil, what you know to be wrong. You can only have the desperate confusion and longing and the chasing of phantom goodness in its human form."[19]

For Louis, and for the vampire experience as Rice shapes it here, all that is left is despair because there can never be an answer to the guilt at the heart of their existence. Unless some sort of universal truth defines sin and provides an answer for it, then guilt has no real substance—and thus no remedy when felt. In the first of the Vampire Chronicles, Rice maintains the spiritual aspects present in the figure of the vampire that were established in *Dracula*, but places those spiritual needs in a fictional universe that has no Christian answers.

Rice published her second Vampire Chronicle, *The Vampire Lestat*, in 1985, several years after *Interview with the Vampire*. It marks a shift in mood and scope from the first novel. The central figure is, of course, Lestat—and his characterization in this novel is significantly different from the previous one. This change can be explained by the shift in point of view. The second novel is narrated by Lestat, who claims that Louis's version of his character in *Interview* is skewed. Rice says in *Conversations with Anne Rice* that the perspective in her second novel came from "wanting to give the strong, independent, atheistic, child-of-nobody point of view in comparison to Louis's."[20] Whatever the reason for the shift, Lestat in this book and those that follow is no longer the conscienceless and superficial figure he was in the first novel. Like Louis, Lestat struggles with guilt over his nature, although his response is rebellious freedom more often than despair. While Louis falls into an endless brooding and wandering, Lestat channels his guilt into an act of rebellion by becoming a celebrity and breaking vampire law by speaking openly about his own nature and the vampire stories he has learned.

Like Louis, Lestat has religious experience in his human past. He wanted to become a priest as a boy, although the spirituality of his youth tends more toward moral behavior than a vibrant religious life: "I wanted to be enclosed forever with people who believed I could be good if I wanted to be."[21] Like Louis, when he is young, he engages in spiritual questioning—he debates with his friend Nicolas over whether death ends with God or with nothingness. And, like Louis, his entering into the vampire state is connected, at least for a moment in his own consciousness, with crossing over to the devil's side. When confronted with his vampire attacker, Lestat explains that he *has* to believe that God exists and he makes the sign of the cross. He exclaims as the vampire takes him, "Then the devil reigns in heaven and heaven is hell."[22] While not as gloomy as Louis, Lestat deals with many of the same spiritual questions that Louis does in the previous novel.

Although Lestat is much less angst-ridden than many of those who surround him, as the novels continue he becomes absorbed with deeper and deeper questions about his existence, and the lack of answers sometimes cripples him and leads him into a state of paralysis. He too recognizes the in-between nature of vampires—having the fundamental nature of a killer but the emotional experiences of a human. It is primarily Lestat's ability to live in the "now," to enjoy experiences as they are offered, that allows him to overcome the vampire angst more than others. He says to Gretchen in *The Tale of the Body Thief,* "My greatest sin has always been that I have a wonderful time being myself. My guilt is always there; my moral abhorrence for myself is always there; but I have a good time. I'm strong; I'm a creature of great will and passion."[23] Lestat is a dynamic character who changes based on context and situations, but he stands out because of his ability to move beyond the angst even though he often suffers from the guilt and existential crisis that Louis does.

The doomed nihilism of Louis is replaced primarily with Lestat's "Savage Garden" philosophy, a name that calls on the wild beauty of the natural world and reflects the worldview itself. This philosophy acknowledges the lack of real meaning in the world and establishes a secular morality that makes aesthetic truths the only ones of value. Lestat says, "A thousand other things can be said about the world, but only aesthetic principles can be verified, and these things alone remain the same."[24] While this worldview gives Lestat more satisfaction than Louis's eternal despair, it does not satisfy Lestat for long—as he eventually loses his faith in the Savage

Garden as he is confronted more and more with spiritual realities in the later novels.

Pagan Roots of Vampire History

Lestat's search for answers about his vampire nature leads him back in history, earlier than the Christian era. Marius, the Roman vampire who values reason and wisdom, connects Lestat's Savage Garden with pagan myths and history in *The Vampire Lestat*. He says, "*We* never served the Christian God. That you can put out of your mind right now." And he follows this claim by alluding to more primitive, more ancient truth than the culture that produced Christianity when he refers to the Druids who turned him into a vampire:

> We are older than that, Lestat. The men that made me were worshipers of gods, true. And they believed in things that I did not believe. But their faith hearkened back to a time long before the temples of the Roman Empire, when the shedding of innocent human blood could be done on a massive scale in the name of good. And evil was the drought and the plague of the locust and the death of the crops. I was made what I am by these men in the name of good.[25]

Lestat, through Marius's explanations, is able to make the connection between pagan myth and the vampire nature. In this context, through the far-ranging truths that Marius teaches him, Lestat learns a key piece of vampire history, the existence of the Mother and Father of vampires, Akasha and Enkil, ancient ones from the early Egyptian era who survive in nearly suspended animation but whose fate determines the fate of all other vampires. The original vampires. This history leads back into the pagan world, in which the vampires were associated with Isis and Osiris by the Egyptians, Dionysus by the Greeks, and the dark gods by the Keltoi (the Celts). Marius explains that it is only with the birth of Christianity that vampires were connected to Satan. They were never considered evil before the Christians made them so.

Marius explains to Lestat the connection between the Mother and Father and the nature of vampires themselves, once again concluding that the nature of a vampire is a spiritual one. He says, "And then it even made sense that we could all be connected to the Mother and the Father because this thing was spiritual, and had no bodily limits except the limits of the individual bodies in which it had gained control"—it was "vine" and vampires the "flowers."[26] Vampire history is connected to ancient pagan religions, clearly distinguished from the Christian world—despite the allusion to Christ's analogy of the vine and the branches (John 15). A relativistic worldview is established throughout the novel—as each vampire's belief system is connected to the age and culture in which they were born and raised. Marius, for instance, is still infected by Western ideas despite knowledge of pagan roots of his vampire existence. He says,

> And though these gods had been revealed to me by Akasha in all their grandeur and mystery, I found them appalling. I could not now or ever embrace them and I knew that the philosophies that proceeded from them or justified them would never justify my killing, or give me consolation as a Drinker of the Blood. Mortal or immortal, I was of the West. And I loved the ideas of the West. And I should always *be guilty* of what I did.[27]

This is a fascinating complexity in the nature of Rice's vampire. Rice puts the vampire guilt in a larger historical context and provides a convincing explanation for it. In *The Vampire Lestat*, the concept of guilt—shaped in so many ways by the

Christian worldview—is itself questioned and thus has less power than in the previous *Interview*.

The pagan roots of vampire history are more fully developed in the next novel, *The Queen of the Damned*. Lestat wakes Akasha, the Mother, and she begins a mission of cleansing the world by destroying most of the men, who she believes are responsible for the evil in the world. She sees her place in history as absolute and universal. She says to Lestat, "I am your true Mother, the Mother who will never abandon you, and I have died and been reborn, too. All the religions of the world, my prince, sing of you and of me."[28] In addition to the pagan connections, Akasha's insistence here links her, in a demonic rather than holy way, with the Virgin Mary, and Lestat therefore with Christ. When Lestat questions her morality, she makes it clear that her perspective goes beyond paganism—she sees herself as the arbiter of truth: "'In the name of *my* morality!' she answered, the faint little smile as beautiful as before. 'I am the reason, the justification, the right by which it is done.'"[29] Marahet, an ancient vampire whose history is irrevocably tied to Akasha's own, understands Akasha's agenda and tells her that it will be the beginning of a new religion, "a new wave of superstition and sacrifice and death,"[30] and this is clearly understood in the scope of the novel as a negative thing. Established religious order is destructive and repressive for Rice, no matter how far-ranging the rationale for it.[31] When Mekare moves to fulfill her prophecy of destroying Akasha, she is covered with mud—emphasizing her connection with nature and the earth. So nature itself rises up to destroy another "god" who would impose an abstract, limited religious code on the world.

What we see in *The Queen of the Damned* is something we also see reflected in later novels—a fictional form of syncretism. In some ways at least, various religions and sources of spirituality are unified as various channels for the same basic truths. Rice herself has said that she thinks the vampire is "an echo of the lusty old gods" or a "disguised image of a vegetation god [like Osiris or Dionysus] that's been inverted and misunderstood."[32] As Bette R. Roberts explains in her critical overview of Rice's work, by connecting the history of vampires to pagan beliefs, Rice "legitimizes vampirism as another myth."[33] Lestat's conclusions after his experiences with Akasha are as follows: "Maharet was right. No room for us; no room for God or the Devil; it should be metaphor—the supernatural—whether it's High Mass at St. Patrick's Cathedral or Faust selling his soul in an opera, or a rock star pretending to be the Vampire Lestat."[34] While spirituality is a genuine human/vampire experience, when it takes concrete form in the world—in organized religion—its consequences are inevitably negative. In one of the later novels, *Merrick*, when Merrick is trying to summon Claudia's ghost, she calls on Papa Legba, St. Peter, the angels, Zoroaster, and others—conflating Christianity with other forms of spirituality. We see in these novels an affirmation of spirituality but a resistance to affirm a particular outgrowth of that experience. This gives the novels more spiritual content than *Interview with the Vampire*, but takes them farther outside of a Christian worldview.

God Incarnate

Throughout the Chronicles, we see a recurring comparison between the nature of the vampire and the nature of God himself. As early as *Interview*, Lestat makes the connection: "God kills, and so shall we; indiscriminately He takes the richest and the poorest, and so shall we; for no creatures under God are as we are, none so like Him as ourselves, dark angels not confined to the stinking limits of hell but wandering His earth and all its kingdoms."[35] Later in that novel, Louis has a powerful experience in St. Louis Cathedral, just before he kills the priest. He looks around at the religious icons and sees them all as "lifeless" and "dead." He sees a vision of himself walking up to the altar and treading on the wafers of the Sacrament. His conclusion from the vision is clear to him: "God did not live in this church; these statues gave an image to nothingness. *I* was the supernatural in this cathedral."[36] The early novels seem to disregard the presence or existence of God in any form—although he's never far from the consciousness of the characters. The vampire becomes the supernatural element that works into Rice's explorations of theology. In later novels, however, Rice puts God more and more at issue. In *Tale of the Body Thief*, David Talbot's theory is that God has a body and therefore God must be flawed. Although Rice's conclusions are never clear or unambiguous, they tend to focus on God as incarnate—that is, God in a bodily form.

It is in *Memnoch the Devil* that theology and Rice's exploration of the person of God come to a head. Memnoch, otherwise known as the Devil, comes to either tempt or enlighten Lestat, and from the beginning Lestat makes the experience universal, saying directly on the first pages that his experience is a human one—it could have happened to a human just as easily as a vampire. He encounters the Christian character Dora, who has a television ministry and genuinely believes in her teaching. Her gospel message is people-oriented and focuses on incarnational theology. She says, "And what is the true message of Christ! . . . That Christ is in every stranger you meet, the poor, the hungry, the sick, the people next door!"[37] So the focus for her, and for the central message of the novel, is that an abstract theology or spirituality can never be constructive. Spiritual truths must take material, human form in order to have real meaning.

Memnoch takes Lestat on a tour through hell and heaven throughout the span of the novel. Ostensibly these spiritual experiences are genuine, although even at the end their meaning and purpose is questioned. It is therefore hard to draw complete conclusions about the theology presented in the novel, since we do not really know whether Memnoch's lessons are real ones or an elaborate deception. However, there are certain things Lestat takes away from the experience that are real and, at least in his perspective, unquestionable. All of those have to do with the human face of God and religion.

In an early scene in *Memnoch the Devil*, Lestat walks into Roger's—his latest victim's—house and finds rooms full of religious objects and icons. The first thing he smells is something "dead," but the religious symbols in this novel are neither empty nor dead, as they are in earlier books. An icon is defined for us by the character of David Talbot as "the work of God. A revelation in material form,"[38] and the focus on icons, including the icon central to the plot of *Memnoch*, the veil of Veronica with the imprint of Christ's face, leads into the novel's more significant theological theme—which has to do with religion in material, human form.

As Memnoch takes Lestat on a cosmic journey, his message inverts traditional Christian theology. The cosmology developed in the novel shapes a history of heaven and hell that fits into the vampire mythology established in the early novels. Memnoch claims that he himself hates evil and that, if God gets his way, evil will destroy the world. According to the devil, Memnoch is responsible for human civilization and higher knowledge, a consequence of Memnoch's interest in human experience—something God himself lacks. According to his story, it was Memnoch who encouraged God to take human form so he could experience what it means to be human and therefore have sympathy with mortals. The cosmology set up in the novel is certainly an inversion of traditional Christian truth, but because of the ambiguity surrounding Memnoch's purposes, it is not clear how much Lestat and the reader are supposed to believe.

What is more essential to the narrative is the way Lestat deals with being bombarded with all of these cosmic "truths." Before he accepts Memnoch's proposal to show him heaven and hell, Lestat tries to work out his confusion with Dora. When Dora asks him whether or not he thinks God would "let people be tricked into Hell," he responds, "I'm not people, Dora. I'm what I am. I don't mean to draw any parallels with God in my repetitive epithets. I only mean I'm evil. Very evil. I know I am. I have been since I started to feed on humans. I'm Cain, the slayer of his brothers."[39] He later admits that he doesn't know why God hasn't already put him into hell for his sins. His guilt is fully at issue in this novel, and it increases the urgency of Lestat's need to understand the truth of his experiences. Shortly after his admission of guilt, he comes to a noteworthy conclusion: "It's not that God is dead in the twentieth century. It's that everybody hates Him!"[40] With his initial impressions of God and Memnoch's insistent questioning of God's wisdom and goodness, it seems that Lestat is set up to reject God and embrace the Devil's purposes.

That is not what happens, however—at least not clearly so. When Lestat is taken by Memnoch to heaven and is confronted with the image of God's face, it is a powerful and shattering experience. Because God goes against all of Lestat's expectations. God doesn't judge or condemn Lestat. Instead, he asks, "You would never be my adversary, would you? You wouldn't, would you? Not you, Lestat, no, not you!" Lestat's silent and ambiguous response is simply an exclamation: "*My God.*"[41] It is the human face of God that means so much to Lestat—that and the plea that implies Lestat's nature is not what he always believed. Much later in the novel, Lestat is confronted with God on the cross. And here he has his most visceral experience of the divine, when God tells Lestat, "The blood. Taste it. Taste the Blood of Christ."[42] In a literal picture of the Sacrament of Holy Communion, the vampire literally drinks of Christ's blood. It is only when God is in human, bodily form that Lestat finds any connection to him at all—and the bodily experience of drinking of his blood is the most concrete and transforming experience of all. While obviously a lot of Christians have had problems with the novel and particularly the scene where Lestat literally drinks of Christ's blood, it is an essential image in terms of developing Rice's spiritual themes. And Rice herself says, in a comment included on her website's page on *Memnoch the Devil*, "This is the most spiritual and most religious of the Vampire Chronicles, a real stepping stone for me in my return to Christ."[43] A careful reading of the novel, particularly in the context of the entire series, will reveal plenty of evidence for her claim.

Lestat's powerful experience encountering Christ on the cross does not answer all of the questions, however, for Lestat or the readers of the novel. In the climax, Christ gives Lestat the veil of Veronica, and Lestat manages to escape with it, although he has to evade Memnoch's attempt to get it back and in the process loses his eye. It is the veil, the icon, the material revelation of God, that highlights the various characters' responses to God's nature. Dora understands the experience as proof of God having won and the Devil being defeated. She takes the veil and begins a whole new religious movement with it. Armand's response is even more dramatic. He too sees it as a sign from God, and he goes to his death in response to it: "'I will bear witness. I will stand here with my arms outstretched,' he cried, 'and when the sun rises, my death shall confirm the miracle.'" Then Armand adds, "Bear witness, this sinner dies for Him!"[44] But Lestat cannot respond as unambiguously. He cannot understand whose will is being carried out through the events. He wonders if he is God's fool or the Devil's fool, asking "Did I serve God? Is that possible? A God I still hate?"[45] But things are turned around again when Memnoch sends him his thanks and Lestat's lost eye, implying that the events of the novel were what Memnoch intended all along. This Lestat cannot accept, preferring to be tricked by God rather than by the Devil. In *Blackwood Farm*, he summarizes his confusion over the event: "If I only knew that Memnoch the Devil and those who came after him had shown me truths! It would all be a different matter and I could somehow save my soul!"[46] But he cannot be sure of any of it and so the theological nature of the universe in Rice's novels is always in doubt.

Memnoch ends with Lestat's declaration of himself. It is entirely in keeping with Lestat's character, as he's the vampire who has always been able to live in the present, even as he deals with his guilt and the questions about his existence. Some of the last lines of the novel give us his conclusions: "I am the Vampire Lestat. This is what I saw. This is what I heard. This is what I know! This is *all* I know."[47] The truth as he understands it is filtered through his own experience, and so again the human aspect of religion is all that we are left with at the end. It is God Incarnate that matters to Rice and who moves her vampires to spiritual revelation.[48]

In Riley's *Conversations with Anne Rice*, Rice makes a fascinating comment about the secular impulse of her writing. She says, "Yes, but I see the best ideas as those that have come out of listening to the flesh very closely."[49] She then juxtaposes this impulse with the Catholic Church's (supposed) condemnation of the flesh as evil and says she believes the opposite of the church—that value and wisdom can be found through the flesh. We can see this worked out in her novels in her emphasis on the incarnate God and theme of transcendence through love.

Transcendent Love

Throughout the Vampire Chronicles, the vampires deal with guilt, existential angst, and ambiguous spiritual and theological experiences. And the primary way any of the characters move beyond their guilt and angst is through love. Even from the beginning of *Interview*, Louis's love for Babette gave his vampire life some sort of purpose and meaning. When he and Lestat change Claudia into a vampire, their "family" gives a certain kind of meaning to their existence. It is clear that Louis loves Lestat as well as Claudia.[50] And it takes a while for different kinds of dissatisfaction to force the three of them apart into a lonelier condition. When Louis attacks and kills the vampires of the *Theatre de Vampire* in Paris after they destroyed Claudia, he admits, "And they are the only deaths I have caused in my long life which are both exquisite and good."[51] It is his love for Claudia that changes the nature of his actions, moving them from guilt to meaning.

Lestat too, from the beginning, is defined by love. He falls in love quickly, passionately, and with both male and female characters. Throughout the Chronicles, we see him fall in love with Louis, with Armand, with Marius, with Gretchen, with Dora, with Rowen, and with many others—mostly vampires but not exclusively so. And it is through the act of loving that he finds meaning in the world. It may only be a temporary solace, but any sort of solace in an angst-filled existence is worthwhile.

In *The Vampire Armand*, Rice continues to explore issues of the spirit and the flesh and similarly concludes that love leads to meaning for existence. The novel begins with the image of Lestat lying on the floor of a chapel in front of a crucifix, immobile and evidently overcome with his spiritual experiences with Memnoch. Armand is the main character of the novel, as the title indicates. And his reflections on his life are prompted by a question from David Talbot, asking why Armand attempted to go to his death when confronted with Christ's icon, the veil of Veronica. Armand's life story and experiences are even more sensual than those of the vampires in the earlier novels—sensual both in the sexual sense and in the focus on art. The events of Armand's life return to Rice's emphasis on love, developing it even more clearly than before. Marius connects love to Christianity and religion very clearly when he tells Armand, "That which was good among the ancients is now rediscovered, and given a new form. You ask me, is Christ the Lord? I say, Amadeo, that He can be, for He never taught anything Himself but love, or so His Apostles, whether they know it or not, have led us to believe."[52] When the sufferings in his life lead Armand to doubt any higher purpose, he converts to the negative picture of organized religion in the Children of Darkness, moving away from Marius's lessons of beauty and love.

When his story reaches the present and his confrontation with the veil, Armand explains his dramatic response by the recognition of Christ's face: "His face, His manly Face infused with the Divine, my tragic Lord gazing at me from my Mother's arms in the frozen sludge of the long-ago street of Podil, my loving Lord in bloody Majesty." And then he says, "Cast me into Hell, Oh Lord, if that is Your will. You have given me Heaven. You have shown me Your Face. And Your Face was human."⁵³ Just as Lestat goes through the visceral experience of drinking from Christ, Armand drinks from Lestat and, in that act, is confronted with Christ himself. He is physically thrown back by the spiritual experience, and he knows it is a result of Christ's presence. His final conclusions are much clearer and more straightforward than Lestat's, but they also focus on the merely human aspect of religion. He explains that Christ isn't theological to him, but rather Christ is his brother: "Yes. That is what He was, my brother, and the symbol of all brothers, and that is why He was the Lord, and that is why His core is simply love."⁵⁴ While Armand can articulate a clearer understanding of what he believes than Lestat ever does, both of them value the same aspect of Christianity and the person of God. That is, God's human face.

Many readers were not pleased with Rice's novels transforming from angst-ridden drama to deep spiritual reflection. This becomes obvious in the first chapter of her final Vampire Chronicle, *Blood Canticle*, where Lestat explains himself in metanarrative, claiming that readers complained about his shift in focus from the early novels to the later ones. He summarizes reader response in this way: "We didn't tell you to go to Heaven and Hell! We want you to be the fancy fiend!"⁵⁵ Then he claims that he is back in a novel that fuses the rebellious mood of the early books with the spiritual meditations of the later ones. He begins, however, by a focus on spirituality by claiming he wants to be a saint, a refrain he returns to throughout the novel. While we certainly see more rebellious posturing from Lestat in this novel, Rice is true to the character development in the previous novels. Lestat hasn't forgotten or ignored all of his spiritual reflections and experiences. And his conclusions in this novel most purely highlight the way Rice melds the earthly and the spiritual in the figure of the vampire—God and human both.[56]

In this novel, we do see Lestat closer to a clear answer than he ever was before. In response to the question of whether he still believes in the Savage Garden aesthetic amorality, Lestat claims that what has replaced that belief is "Belief in The Maker . . . who put it all together with love and purpose. What else?"[57] But his conclusions, and the conclusions of the Vampire Chronicles as a whole, are not traditionally Christian or even entirely spiritual. The final answer is love. Lestat's final spiritual search is one in search of love: "And my mind cast back over the centuries, like the mechanism of conscience determined to ferret out sin, only it searched for moments of *pure love*."[58] He has an almost transcendent moment with Rowen at the climax of the novel, in which the world is transformed for him—and that moment is defined by love: "The world reborn in love, and common things overlayered with common despair leapt into colors brilliant and irresistible."[59] The final act we see him perform is one of almost pure sacrificial love, in letting Rowen go because that will be in her best interest instead of claiming her for himself like he desperately wants. He recognizes the irony of his gesture of selflessness—being a vampire, a sinner, a self-proclaimed agent of the Devil. But he loves her, and he knows her life will be better if he does not try to keep her.

And it is clear he cannot remain in that moment or that selfless attitude for very long. His nature is what it is and is not going to change despite his transcendent experiences. And this is the way Rice is able to fuse Lestat's characteristic wandering rebellion with a deep exploration of Christian themes and truths. He ends this novel with a declaration of his evil nature and his endless search for an answer to his guilt:

Be gone from me, oh mortals who are pure of heart. Be gone from my thoughts, oh souls that dream great dreams. Be gone from me, all hymns of glory. I am the magnet for the damned. At least for a little while. And then my heart cries out, my heart will not be still, my heart will not give up, my heart will not give in—

—the blood that teaches life will not teach lies, and love becomes again my reprimand, my goad, my song.[60]

Again, the best conclusion the vampire can come to in order to understand and find meaning in the world is love—and through love the vampire might be able to understand his true nature.

In her most recent novels on the life of Christ, written after her return to Christ, Rice develops many of the same themes she does in the Vampire Chronicles but puts them in the context of a Christ-centered worldview. In the Christ the Lord series, *Out of Egypt* and *The Road to Cana*, she focuses on the human aspects of Christ's life, his childhood and young adulthood and his growing recognition of himself as divine Son of God. She emphasizes his sensory experiences: eating, lying in the grass, gazing at the natural world and other humans. And she doesn't overlook the very human desires for love and family. Thus she navigates a tight balance between a portrait of Christ as fully human and a portrait of him as fully God. While she played with the same balance in her vampire characters—between their carnal and their spiritual or supernatural natures—the themes seem to find its culmination in her portrait of Christ. If the Vampire Chronicles reveal various ways in which Rice worked through spiritual issues through the figure of the vampire, the Christ the Lord novels show where all of those reflections led her.

Rice's imaginative expression in the figure of the vampire is not wholly secular, although she herself claims that it is.

In the figure of the vampire, spiritual reflections are real, and spiritual experiences are also genuine. But the conclusions have to focus on the world, on the human—clearly represented in the figure of the vampire. And so in Rice we see a clear transition from the theological purpose of the vampire in *Dracula* and the wholly secular pictures we will see in vampire stories that follow.

4

Buffy the Vampire Slayer

Sin and Sacrifice, Postmodern Style

It's not the demon in me that needs killing, Buffy. It's the man.

Angel in "Amends"
(*Buffy the Vampire Slayer*, season 3)

Just before the "Scooby Gang" marches off to stop their fourth or fifth apocalypse in the season 5 finale episode of *Buffy the Vampire Slayer*, Xander (Nicholas Brendon) asks why the fallen hell-god Glory needs to use blood to perform her world-ending ritual. Spike (James Marsters), a vampire kept from doing active harm by an implanted chip in his head, gives the television show's answer to the literal and symbolic significance of blood. He says, "Blood is life, lackbrain. Why do you think we eat it? It's what keeps you going, makes you warm, makes you hard, makes you other than dead. 'Course it's her blood."[1] This reference to the verse in Deuteronomy

(12:23) is a direct connection to *Dracula*, as we saw in the earlier chapter. In *Dracula*, the vampire's unnatural desire to feed on blood is a perversion of Holy Communion and a means of human damnation. Throughout the seven seasons of *Buffy the Vampire Slayer*, blood functions with similar symbolic significance, but the symbolism is made more complex by its presence in a postmodern show that ultimately validates multiple worldviews.

In *Buffy*, blood represents life, power, and sexuality. It also represents death. Feeding on blood implies damnation and at the same time a desirable intimacy. Spilling blood is negative as portrayed in the show—violence always has serious consequences. But spilling blood is also set up as a mission, a divine calling. Because of the complexity of treating as a single story 144 different episodes that aired over seven years—episodes written, directed, produced, and performed by hundreds of different artists—my discussion of some of the major themes in *Buffy* will be streamlined by necessity. I will focus primarily on episodes written and directed by Joss Whedon, the show's creator and central visionary. Even with this focus, the spiritual and religious themes in Buffy are complex enough to warrant an entire book.[2] But in this chapter I will begin to analyze the show, arguing for its place in the process of secularization of the vampire figure.

Buffy the Vampire Slayer explores many of the same themes we saw in *Dracula*, including sin, guilt, spiritual warfare, and Christian iconography. The show actually goes deeper into the theological themes of grace, forgiveness, sacrifice, and free will than Stoker tackled, but—unlike Dracula—*Buffy* is not a Christian story. Like Anne Rice, the makers of *Buffy* delve into the consciousness of the vampire himself, although most of the focus is on the vampire hunters. And, also like in Rice, a vampire—at least an ensouled vampire—has the potential to feel guilt and to regret the harm he has done. The secularization in *Buffy* occurs not by removing the vampire from a religious context, as we will see happens in later examples like the Sookie Stackhouse and Twilight books, but by layering other forms of spirituality, philosophy, and worldview on top of the Christian one. Ultimately, *Buffy* is postmodern, skeptical of any unifying, grand narratives, both validating and questioning multiple worldviews through the image of the vampire even while affirming the Christian theological roots of the vampire myth. In my analysis of the show, I will explore how *Buffy* uses the nature of the vampire to explore what it means to be a sinner. Then I will touch on some of the spiritual answers to sin offered by the show's narrative: sacrifice, love, and grace. And finally I will argue that, despite using the vampire as a site for these theological reflections, the show's final conclusions are primarily secular ones.

The Vampire as Sinner

Although the word *sin* is rarely used in *Buffy the Vampire Slayer*, the picture created by the portrait of the vampire on the show very clearly reflects traditional understandings of sin. In its exploration of the vampire's nature as sinful, the show reflects many of the same ideas we saw in *Dracula*. While Rice invests her vampires with endless guilt, the source of that guilt is not always clearly defined as sin—and even when it is, the truth of the claims is questionable. This is not true of *Buffy*. In *Buffy*, the vampires are unquestionably sinners, and neither the audience nor other characters question that unless it is for rhetorical or manipulative purposes.[3]

In the first episode of the series, "Welcome to the Hellmouth," Buffy's Watcher Giles (Anthony Stewart Head), fulfilling his role as "exposition guy,"[4] sets up the nature of vampires in the show's universe (the Buffyverse, as it is referred to by fans and by scholars who study the show). Giles explains:

> This world is older than you know. Contrary to popular mythology, it did not begin as a paradise. For untold eons, demons walked the earth. They made it their home, their . . . their hell. But in time, they lost their purchase on this reality. . . . The books tell the last demon to leave this reality fed off a human, mixed their blood. He was a human form possessed, infected by the demon's soul.[5]

As it is explained here, a vampire is simply a human body taken over by a demon soul. While mirroring something of what the sin nature did to humans, in itself this portrait of vampires is not a particularly good reflection of sinful humans—as vampires are missing the key piece that makes them human—the human soul.

Vampires very clearly are not human. Buffy (Sarah Michelle Gellar) and the others have no qualms about killing vampires, turning them into dust. And over and over again killing vampires and killing humans are considered very different things, with entirely different sets of consequences.[6] So the run-of-the-mill vampire on *Buffy* is not a particularly good picture of sin. Rather, they are monsters who must merely be killed and therefore are not complex portraits of anything.

We do see, in the first season, some similarities with Stoker's portrait of vampires in *Dracula*. Just as Count Dracula is portrayed, in many ways, as having characteristics that are perversions of Christianity, so The Master (Mark Metcalf)—the first season's "Big Bad," the main villain—is quite clearly a perversion of a Christian figure. More than other vampires on the show, The Master is religious. He speaks in religious language ("As it is written, so shall it be" and "Here endeth the lesson . . ."[7]). He waits for The Anointed One. He surrounds himself with candles and ritual and accepts "offerings" from his followers. And he is waiting for a kind of resurrection from the underground prison in which he is trapped. In "Nightmares," he talks about the things he fears and walks over to a large cross, declaring that it cannot "master" him as he grabs it and his hand starts to smoke.[8]

The Master is probably the most blatantly religious of the vampires on the show, all of his religious language and feeling being a subversion or perversion of traditional Christianity. Like Dracula, his appearance is even a mirror of his nature. Unlike most of the vampires on *Buffy*, who retain their human appearance until they prepare to feed, The Master's demon nature has permanently affected his appearance. As Matthew Pateman argues, his appearance is an homage to Friedrich Wilhelm Murnau's *Nosferatu* (1922). At the beginning of season 2, the vampire Spike makes his first appearance, announcing that he's ready for "a little less ritual and a little more fun."[9] From that point on, the vampires on the show generally became less religious and ritualistic, although there were always a few exceptions.

With the development of the character of Angel (David Boreanaz), the vampire with a soul, the show was able to more deeply explore the nature of sin. In vengeance for his torture and killing of the daughter of a gypsy clan, the vampire Angelus was cursed with his human soul again—making him suffer endlessly out of guilt for all his evil deeds as a vampire. The guilt connects him to Anne Rice's vampires, but Angel's guilt is more concretely theological than the existential angst suffered by Lestat and Louis. Angel's soul gives him free will and the ability to do good, something the other vampires on *Buffy* do not possess. But his soul also tortures him—he says, "A hundred years, just hanging out, feelin' guilty. I really honed my brooding skills."[10]

It is through Angel during the first three seasons of *Buffy* that we see the potential for the image of the vampire to provide a metaphor for a human cursed with a sin nature. Angel doesn't just feel guilty because of his past deeds. He also has to constantly struggle against his vampire nature. When he and Buffy first kiss in the episode "Angel," he morphs into his vampire form, his true nature coming to the surface when overcome with passion or the desire to feed. And when Buffy asks him in that same episode why he didn't tell her he wasn't the one who attacked her mother, he admits, "But I wanted to. I can walk like a man, but I'm not one. I wanted to kill you tonight."[11] When he is ranting about his guilt in the season 3 episode "Amends," he admits that he wants Buffy so much he is tempted to take her. Even though it might cost him his soul, "a part of [him] doesn't care."[12] The constant struggle between his evil nature and his human soul is what defines Angel, and the show never makes it easy for him. At the end of the episode "Angel," the last shot is of Angel's chest, with an image of Buffy's cross burnt into his skin, a fitting picture of the conflict between sin and righteousness in his character.

The portrait of sin through Angel's character is not black-and-white or simplistic. Authentic complexity in the handling of themes is one of the things *Buffy* always does well. The responsibility for evil deeds is never wiped away, even if the doer has repented or changed. An excellent example of this is in the season 2 finale episode "Becoming." Midway through the season, Buffy and Angel consummate their love and, after achieving a moment of real happiness and contentment, Angel loses his soul, becoming a remorseless monster again. In "Becoming," Buffy and the others debate over whether or not to try to restore his soul. Buffy, still loving him, wants to do so. But Xander insists that Angel doesn't deserve it:

Xander: Hi! For those of you who have just tuned in, everyone here is a crazy person. So this spell might restore Angel's humanity? Well, here's an interesting angle. Who cares?

Buffy: I care.

Xander: Is that right.

Giles: Let's not lose our perspective here, Xander.

Xander: I'm Perspective Guy. Angel's a killer.

Willow: Xander . . .

Buffy: It's not that simple.

Xander: What? All is forgiven? I can't believe you people!

. . . .

Willow (to Buffy): What do you wanna do?

Buffy: I—I don't know. What happened to Angel wasn't his fault.

Xander: Yeah, but what happened to Ms. Calendar is. You can paint this any way you want. But the way I see it is that you wanna forget all about Ms. Calendar's murder so you can get your boyfriend back.[13]

This conversation and those surrounding it provide a remarkably astute theological exploration of human sin nature as seen in the Bible. As Buffy says, Angel isn't to blame for what happened to him—for becoming a vampire and then for later losing his soul and becoming a monster again. But Xander isn't wrong when he says that Angel's murder of Jenny Calendar *was* his fault. Despite his inability to control his vampire nature without a soul, Angel is still responsible for the evil deeds he commits. The Bible teaches that we are incapable of not sinning but we are still responsible for the sin we commit. The show's distinct portrait of vampire nature provides a lens through which to explore these issues, and it does so more deeply than *Dracula*.

The only other vampire on the show through which we see the issue of sin similarly explored is Spike. In season 4, Spike is captured by the Initiative, a covert military group assigned to hunt and research monsters. While he is captured, the Initiative plants a chip in his head that prevents him from doing harm to anything human by causing Spike great pain when he attempts it. In season 4, Spike is like a chained animal or an imprisoned serial killer (an analogy Buffy uses in the next season)—wanting to do evil but physically prevented from doing so.

In season 5, however, his character starts to change. He falls in love with Buffy and has the desire to do good because of it. We see him perform several acts that appear to be noble—he refuses to tell Glory about Dawn's being the Key, even when she brutally tortures him, and he risks death in the final fight against Glory in order to protect Dawn. Season 5 seems to allow the possibility that vampires do in fact have free will and are capable of doing good if given enough incentive. Either the writing and the development of themes in the series is somewhat inconsistent or viewers are supposed to interpret Spike's behavior in season 5 as ultimately selfish,[14] but season 6 returns to the show's original vampire mythology: it is only with a human soul that vampires are capable of doing real good.

In season 6, Spike's love for Buffy is consummated, but their sexual relationship is made up of violence, mutual selfishness, and unhealthy interdependence—both of them seeking only to use the other rather than relating out of love, respect, or care. When Spike attempts to rape Buffy in the episode "Seeing Red," the creators seem to give their conclusive answer about Spike's nature. No matter how much he wants to do good, he is incapable of being anything other than evil as a vampire, unless he has a human soul. So, in the finale of that season, he goes in search of a soul—facing a number of overwhelming challenges in order to finally have his soul restored.

When his soul is restored, Spike goes half crazy because of the way it tortures him with his guilt. In the season 7 episode "Beneath You," Buffy realizes during a conversation the two have in a chapel that his soul has been restored. A large cross is featured prominently throughout the conversation, and the spiritual aspects of the conversation are obvious as Spike struggles to understand what it means to have his soul again. At two points, he seems to address God himself, although the moments are ambiguous enough to be interpreted otherwise. He says, "Oh God, I can't . . ." which could be a direct address to God or could be simply an exclamation. And later he looks to the heavens and says, "It's what you wanted, isn't it?" He repeats the question to Buffy, which implies the first question was directed at God. At the end of the conversation, he drapes himself over the cross, sizzling as his skin burns at the contact.[15] His suffering is not really a reflection of Christ, though. He is suffering for his own sins, not the sins of others.

Spike doesn't truly become a hero until the series finale, "Chosen," when he gives up his life, his soul, his existence in order to save other people. The fact that he is consumed in an eruption of light makes it clear that at the end he has chosen to be a true sacrifice, with no question about his actions being selfishly motivated. This could not have happened without a restoration of his soul. His sins are finally burned away in light—a fitting end for the journey of his character.[16] It is, perhaps, unfortunate for the development of this theme throughout the series that *Buffy*'s spinoff series *Angel* brought

Spike's character back the following year, undoing all of the thematic significance of his death in *Buffy*.[17]

Vampires in *Buffy* are given spiritual significance and used to explore the nature of sin, just as they are in *Dracula*. But Buffy goes even farther in exploring theological themes connected to sin—those of sacrifice, love, and grace.

Answers to Sin: Sacrifice, Love, and Grace

Halfway through "Restless," the fourth season finale episode, Giles—at this point fired from both of his positions as librarian and Buffy's Watcher—has a dream, one in the series of dreams that make up the episode. At a booth in a carnival, Giles admonishes Buffy, who in this part of the dream is figuring as his child, on her ability to throw balls at toy vampires. Buffy pouts, tries again, hits the fake vampire, and turns around, expecting praise. "I haven't got any treats," Giles informs her. And when his other companion tells him to "go easy" on Buffy, Giles continues, almost complaining: "This is my business. Blood of the lamb and all that."[18] In an episode where every object, statement, and detail becomes symbolically significant, an episode described by writer/director Joss Whedon as "basically a forty-minute poem," this line points not only to Giles's own ambivalence toward his life's work, but also to the centrality of sacrifice in the series as a whole.[19] Giles's business, and thus the role of the Slayer in the fictional universe, is "the blood of the lamb," is sacrifice. Through seven seasons of action scenes, supernatural crises, and wisecracks, the necessity of sacrifice became the thematic premise of the television show.

Sacrifice in *Buffy* comes in two distinct forms: that of being a "living" sacrifice and that of bloody sacrifice through death. The first kind of sacrifice is explored at some level in nearly every episode of the show. There is a certain degree of sacrifice involved in ordinary living—in dealing with one's responsibilities, in persevering even when things get hard, in handling the struggles life offers with strength and courage. From the very beginning of the show, we can see Buffy trying to deal with her calling as Slayer and all of the extra burdens that come with it. In the series premiere, "Welcome to the Hellmouth," Buffy confronts Giles, who wants her to resume her role as Slayer which she is trying to run away from. She responds to his explanation of how Watchers help to prepare Slayers: "Prepare me for what? For getting kicked out of school? For losing all of my friends? For having to spend all of my time fighting for my life and never getting to tell anyone because I might endanger them? Go ahead! Prepare me."[20] Being a Slayer is only occasionally enjoyable for Buffy. Most of the time she suffers for it—physically, socially, and psychologically. But the show makes it clear that giving up her calling is both cowardly and morally wrong. She is to truly be a living sacrifice, giving of herself for the good of the world.

Buffy is not the only character called to this form of sacrificial living. All of the characters, at one point or another over the seven seasons, are expected to make various forms of sacrifice through their everyday living, in order to do their duty. One of the recurring motifs is the way Giles finds it impossible to have a personal life because of his role as Watcher. Twice throughout the series he tries to form a relationship with a girlfriend, but he fails both times—once because Jenny Calendar gets killed because of her association with him and Buffy, and once because Olivia simply can't deal with the pressures of his position. Giles leaves for England twice in order to try to live his life—but both times he is called back to Sunnydale because he is needed there.

The other characters are in similar positions. Xander explains the difficulty of his role to Dawn in "Potential"—that of being on the sidelines and watching others shine. He poignantly explains that it is much harder not to be chosen, not to have the power. But, because his role is a supportive one, he fulfills it despite the difficulty and often ends up saving the day because of it (as we see in episodes like "The Zeppo"). As the Scooby Gang sings in "Walk through the Fire," in the season 6 musical episode, "Once More, with Feeling," "We'll see it through, it's what we're always here to do, so we will walk through the fire . . ."[21] Perseverance at personal cost is what is required of everyone. A twice repeated refrain is spoken by Buffy in "The Gift" and Dawn in "Once More, with Feeling" and embodies the theme of sacrificial living: "The hardest thing in this world is to live in it."[22]

But living is not the only form of sacrifice explored by the show. The other form is equally prominent and important in the Buffyverse. Bloody sacrifice—the sacrifice of one's life—is just as important as sacrificial living. The series is built around the necessity of death from the very first season. In the season 1 finale, "Prophecy Girl," Buffy finds out that it is prophesied that she will die when she faces The Master. Her first response, naturally enough, is rebellion. She reacts in anger against being ordained to die by an ancient prophecy, and she ends her rant by saying, "Giles, I'm sixteen years old. I don't want to die."

Ultimately she makes the decision to willingly go to her death, because The Master must be stopped and that is her calling and duty as Slayer. The viewers are supposed to think of Christ with Buffy's actions. When she reaches The Master's lair, he says, "But you are not the hunter. You are the lamb." And The Master does in fact kill her (briefly) because Buffy is not strong enough to resist his hypnotic power. Then Xander brings her back to life through his love, commitment, and CPR. Buffy's "resurrection" gives her the necessary power and strength to defeat The Master—she says, "No, no. I feel strong. I feel different"—and the fact that she fights The Master in her prom dress highlights the foundational irony of the series.[23]

At the end of the following season of the show, we see Buffy called to bloody sacrifice again. But this time it is not her own life she must sacrifice: it the life of Angel, whom she loves. After he loses his soul, Angelus, as Angel's evil vampire self is called, starts a campaign of torture against Buffy and her friends. In "Becoming" Buffy's friends rediscover the spell that would curse Angelus again with a soul just as he is about to awaken a demon who will pull the world into a hell dimension: as Buffy says, "the literal kind of 'sucked into hell.'"[24] The potential apocalypse can only be stopped by Angel's blood, which will ritually close the gate between the world and the threatened hell dimension. His blood started the ritual and so only his blood can stop it. So Buffy has to kill not Angelus but Angel. And she does so at great cost. It is clearly the right decision. She has done her duty, done what she needed to do, and sacrificed her personal feelings and Angel's life to save the world.

At the end of season 5, we have a parallel scenario. Some necessary context: to keep a mystical energy force known as the Key safe, a group of monks transform it into human form using Buffy's blood, and recreate memories that cause the world to believe Dawn (Michelle Trachtenberg), the Key, is and always has been Buffy's sister. After a season of searching, a fallen god from a hell dimension, Glory (Claire Kramer), has found the Key, in the form of Dawn, and is planning to use her to open a portal, which will dissolve the walls between all dimensions. In "The Gift," Buffy and her friends must rescue Dawn before Glory goes through with the ritual. In the final moments of the episode, the ritual (performed by draining Dawn's blood) has already started, and the only way to end it and save the world is to stop Dawn's blood—to kill her before the ritual is complete. The similarities with the end of "Becoming" are obvious and intentional. "The Gift" presents another moment where the ritual spilling of blood causes the walls between dimensions to dissolve and another kind of scapegoat—a victim who is literally marginal in the community—to bear the weight of the world's evil. Like Angel, Dawn is halfway between human and something else.

But Buffy is not the same at the end of season 5. And she is no longer willing to sacrifice someone she loves. Since Dawn was made from Buffy, they share the same blood, so Buffy sacrifices herself instead—dying to save Dawn and the rest of the world. There are lingering questions about the nobility of Buffy's actions here, still debated extensively in online discussions. Buffy's duty is to be the Slayer—she is called to fight, not give up her life in the place of Dawn's. And, logically speaking, she can do far more good for the world alive than Dawn can. If the "hardest thing in this world is to live in it," then there is a sense that Buffy's actions in "The Gift" are a kind of surrender. She gives up. However much many viewers judge her for it, the show itself never does so. Her sacrifice was done in love, and that alone gives it value.

In season 2, duty won out over love. But in season 5, love prevailed over duty. The show makes it clear, however, that individuals are called to both. Both love and duty are what lead the characters to sacrifice, and sacrifice is the only successful response to the evil in the world. The love most often explored by the show is not romantic love—although there is certainly plenty of that. The more fundamental love, however, is closer to *agape,* and it is seen in the context of family, friendship, and larger communities. This love is selfless and sacrificial and very often does not end up rewarding the giver. Season 5 prepares the way for Buffy's sacrificial death. In "Intervention" she seeks guidance through a vision quest in the desert, and an image of the First Slayer comes to her and tells her that she is "full of love" and that love will lead her to "her gift." The message is made clear when the vision guide says, "Death is your gift."[25] Buffy doesn't understand the significance until later. But it is this sacrificial love that has value in the series.

We can see this kind of love again at the culmination of season 6. Victory is once more achieved only by love as Xander's love for his best friend, Willow, saves the world. Willow (Alyson Hannigan), channeling unstoppable magics, fueled by grief and the need for vengeance at the death of her lover, Tara, has lost her grip on reality and her humanity. Her actions have the potential to destroy the whole world, which she sees at that moment as a good thing since the world involves so much misery. Xander is the only one who is able to stop her. He has no power other than love.

Willow: You can't stop this.

Xander: Yeah, I get that. It's just, where else am I gonna go? You've been my best friend my whole life. World gonna end . . . where else would I want to be?

Willow: Is this the master plan? You're going to stop me by telling me you love me?

Xander: Well, I was going to walk you off a cliff and hand you an anvil, but it seemed kinda cartoony.

Willow: Still making jokes.

Xander: I'm not joking. I know you're in pain. I can't imagine the pain you're in. And I know you're about to do something apocalyptically evil and stupid, and hey I still want to hang. You're Willow.

71

Willow: Don't call me that!

Xander: The first day of kindergarten, you cried because you broke the yellow crayon, and you were too afraid to tell anyone. You've come pretty far, ending the world, not a terrific notion. But the thing is, yeah. I love you. I loved crayon-breaky Willow and I love scary veiny Willow. So if I'm going out, it's here. If you wanna kill the world, well, then start with me. I've earned that.

Willow: You think I won't?

Xander: It doesn't matter. I'll still love you.[26]

When Willow starts to physically attack him, Xander persists—saying over and over again that he loves her. While duty is always important in *Buffy*, it must be balanced by love and forgiveness.[27]

In a Buffyverse defined by evil and sin that can only be combated through sacrifice, the only grace comes through this kind of love. There are never any easy answers in *Buffy*, but the universe does offer something other than pain and suffering. This is seen most clearly in the Christmas episode "Amends," from season 3. Angel has been sent back from hell by The First Evil in order to kill Buffy. He does, however, still have his soul, so much of the season up to this point is Angel's struggle with his own evil nature. The First Evil, who is "beyond sin, beyond death . . . the thing that darkness fears . . . every being, every thought, every drop of hate," is something Buffy can never kill, can never even begin to fight. The First Evil has convinced Angel that he must either kill Buffy or kill himself, and Angel has resolved to do the latter. He cannot fight his own evil nature, so the only righteous thing he can think of is to die. The situation is hopeless. There is nothing in humanity strong enough, powerful enough to fight evil in its purest form (at least not as The First is depicted in season 3). Angel is waiting for the sun to rise on Christmas morning and kill him. Buffy finds Angel and tries to stop him, telling him to fight, to live, to recognize that everyone is weak, but he still has "the power to do real good, to make amends."[28] Angel, however, recognizing the reality of the situation, counters that "It's not the demon in me that needs killing. . . . It's the man."[29]

The episode provides a rich and perceptive exploration of humanity's sinful nature. It is not just that humans are not strong enough to fight evil in general. They are not strong enough to fight their own sinful nature. Some good can be done, but not all the time, and not enough. Angel, trying to resist Buffy's pleadings, pushes her down violently and asks her, "Am I a thing worth saving, huh? Am I a righteous man?" The answer, of course, is, "No." Buffy continues to try to save him, falling back on the show's consistent moral message that evil can only be fought from within—"Strong is fighting! It's hard, and it's painful, and it's every day. It's what we have to do." This is going back to the idea of sacrificial living. It has worked at other times in the show, but it does not work now. Fighting, even everyday sacrificial living, cannot always or inevitably bring salvation. The sun is about to rise, and with it, Angel will be killed.[30]

Here is one of the rare moments in popular culture in which we can see a pure and unadulterated picture of grace. Evil is too strong. Humans cannot fight it alone. And so we get, at this moment, the answer of the universe to the irresistible pull of The First Evil. It begins to snow on Christmas morning in Sunnydale, California—a freak snowfall over one city in a state faced with a heat wave. What would be a clichéd and shallow contrivance in a more predictable show becomes one of the most powerful moments in the whole run of the show. Because this never happens. Salvation never comes from outside of humanity. And yet, at this moment, it does. As the weatherman says in a radio voice-over, "Sunnydale residents shouldn't expect to see the sun at all today."[31] The sun, which would spell Angel's doom, will not rise at all that Christmas morning. There is a response to evil. It is unlooked for, unasked, unexplainable, and completely inevitable. Like grace, the snow saves Angel's life despite everything he has done and has been.

Theology Secularized

Despite the theological issues and themes explored by the show, *Buffy the Vampire Slayer* certainly isn't a Christian story. The figure of the vampire becomes secularized in the show because of the way it refuses to affirm any definite spiritual reality but instead points toward many of them.

One way in which we see this happen is the consistent questioning of organized religion and Christianity in the series. For the most part, Christian characters on *Buffy* are negative portraits of religious people. This shows up in minor ways, like an offhand moment in "The Freshman," where a proselytizing student approaches Buffy, asking, "Have you accepted Jesus Christ as your personal savior?" Buffy answers with typical flippancy: "Uh, you know I meant to and then I just got really busy."[32] In a larger sense, organized religion and more traditional Christianity is critiqued in season 5 with the Knights of Byzantium, a group of anachronistic warriors fighting a crusade to destroy the Key and thus save the world from the hell-god Glory. While the knights are not evil, they must be fought by Buffy because of their narrow-minded zealotry. They chant, "The Key is the link. The link must be severed. Such is the will of God."[33] And they refuse to acknowledge Dawn's innocence or listen to Buffy's passionate defense against killing her. They all end up dead because of their self-righteous ignorance. They are absolutely committed to their duty and calling, but without love, grace, or understanding. And so the religious portrait they convey is a negative one.

Then, at the end of season 7, we return to the kind of perversion of Christianity we saw in the first season with The Master. This happens in the form of the character Caleb (Nathan Fillion), a former preacher who is now an emissary of The First. In one of his early speeches, in the episode "Dirty Girls," Caleb muses over the wine he is sipping:

> "Drink of this, for it is my blood." You know, I always loved the story of the Last Supper. The body and blood of Christ becoming rich, red wine. I recall, as a boy, though, I couldn't help but think: what would happen if you were at the Last Supper, and you ordered the white? A nice oaky Chardonnay or White Zin . . . I mean, would he make that out of his lymph or some-all? Never did bring it up. Suppose there was a reason why I never spent too long in one parish. Just looking for answers. Just looking for the Lord in the wrong damn places. Then you showed me the light.[34]

The "you" he addresses is The First, in that scene taking the form of Buffy. The First blatantly distinguishes himself from God, but Caleb—still dressed as a preacher—remains a very religious character and a stereotypical Southern hellfire-and-brimstone preacher. So, even while the characterization continues the show's habit of using religion in various forms to express complicated ideas, it also critiques that religion at the same time.

Only occasionally does the show becomes explicit about the Christian God. One such moment reveals as close to an answer as *Buffy* ever comes about how Christianity fits into the Buffyverse. In season 7's "Conversations with Dead People," Buffy begins to talk to a newly risen vampire who happens to be an old classmate of hers, Holden. Atypically, instead of immediately staking him, Buffy has an extended conversation with Holden in which Buffy shares some of what she is struggling with to a companion who is (at least emotionally) safe. During this conversation, they have a brief discussion about God's existence:

> Holden: Oh, my God!
> Buffy: Oh, your God what?
> Holden: Oh, well, you know, not my God, because I defy him and all of his works, but—Does he exist? Is there word on that, by the way?
> Buffy: Nothing solid.[35]

"Nothing solid" seems to be as definitive as the show is willing to be on this subject. And this marks a significant difference between *Buffy the Vampire Slayer* and *Dracula* (and even between *Buffy* and Anne Rice, whose Vampire Chronicles do validate the existence of God in some form). While both use the image of the vampire to explore central theological questions of Christianity, *Dracula* places the vampire within a Christian universe, while *Buffy* constantly questions that reality.

It is not only by questioning Christianity that the vampire in *Buffy* is secularized. More fundamentally, it is the way the show layers multiple worldviews over the one that reflects Christian theology. One of those worldviews is the "new age" paganism explored primarily through Willow in her dealings with Wicca and witchcraft.[36] As with Christianity, the show questions this ideology as much as it affirms it, but its principles run counter in many ways to those of Christianity. Like Anne Rice, the makers of *Buffy* integrate paganism into vampire mythology, but—unlike Rice—they never try to construct a unified mythology in which both make sense. Rather, in *Buffy*, paganism is an alternate worldview that exists at the same time as the Christian worldview but isn't unified or connected.

In the first season, witchcraft is seen from a negative point of view with the episode "The Witch," in which a student's mother resorts to the black arts to live out her own fantasies of being a cheerleader. Because it is selfishly and destructively used, witchcraft in the episode is something that must be fought against. When Jenny Calendar arrives on the scene, defining herself as a "techno-pagan," a more positive perspective on paganism and witchcraft is introduced. Jenny uses modern technology to explore the supernatural world, but admits to not having enough power to be a witch. All of her knowledge of the mystical world, magic, and paganism is used constructively on the show, and she is the one who rediscovers the spell to restore Angel's soul to him at the end of season 2, before she herself is killed by him. Inspired by Jenny, Willow begins dabbling in witchcraft throughout season 3. The potential for harm and misuse is never far from the surface of the show's exploration of these ideas, most often vocalized by Giles. But it is not until season 4 that the pagan worldview truly takes root in the show's development.

During her first year of college, Willow joins a campus Wiccan group and is frustrated by their focus on bake sales rather than genuine power. As Willow says in the episode "Hush," satirizing a lot of popular paganism in our culture: "Blah blah Gaia. Blah blah moon, menstrual lifeforce power thingy. You know after a couple of sessions I was hoping we would get into something real but . . . nowadays every girl with a henna tattoo and a spice rack thinks she's a sister to the Dark Ones."[37] But in the group she meets Tara (Amber

Benson), another witch who, at that point, is more advanced in the arts than Willow herself. Together, they cultivate their witchcraft and develop a romantic relationship.

Lesbianism in the show is intricately connected to Willow's development as a witch. Throughout season 4, her friend's skepticism of Willow's "new thing" is an overlap between their reaction to her as a witch and her as a lesbian. More than once, magic is an analogy for lesbian activity—as we can see at the end of season 5's "Family," where Willow and Tara rise into the air in a romantic dance, and in "Once More, with Feeling," where Tara rises from the bed in what is obviously a sexual experience. It is perhaps not surprising that some viewers saw the portrait of homosexuality on the show as ambiguous and potentially negative, as it is so clearly connected to witchcraft. Magic is never safe in the show, and its portrait is at least sometimes negative. In season 6, Willow gets lost in an addiction to magic and gives in to evil through the black arts. If the analogy with homosexuality was extended, then it too could be implied as being dangerous or destructive.

In the final season, however, the show's conclusions on paganism and witchcraft—as with a lot of other thematic issues—are resolved. After her descent into darkness, Willow fears using magic at all. But she has to throughout the season, and in the end she learns how to use it well. In the last episode, "Chosen," her use of a spell causes her to be transformed by white light, an obvious opposition to the Dark Willow of season 6. She breathes out, "Oh . . . my . . . Goddess," as she is overwhelmed by the magic experience.[38] Paganism and witchcraft are affirmed by the show when used constructively and wisely. It is connected to the earth, to womanhood, to pagan traditions of the supernatural,[39] and it is a worldview that does not line up with the traditional

Christian one also explored by the show. Critics like Zoe-Jane Playden have argued that *Buffy* espouses a feminist spirituality that is connected to pre-Christian religious experience.[40] In fact, both are affirmed and both are questioned by the show, as is typical in a postmodern text.

The structure of the Buffyverse makes it possible to explore and affirm various perspectives and worldviews. There are multiple dimensions, each with different rules and different philosophical foundations. Because of this, it is impossible for one set of truths to define the *Buffy* universe. When she dies after season 5, Buffy goes to what she calls a heaven dimension—clearly delineated from the heaven of Christian tradition. Multiple hell dimensions are explained in the show at various points. And there are also various realities, like the dark reality of "The Wish" in which Buffy never comes to Sunnydale. This reality seems to exist in its own space, since the Willow from that reality is able to enter the known Buffy reality in "Doppelgangland." And throughout season 5, the "Big Bad" Glory is an alternate picture of God. She is a god from a hell dimension and is a portrait of a petty, vindictive, vain, and fatuous god who is nearly all-powerful (her power is limited only by her bodily form) and has regular temper-fits when things don't go her way or people aren't worshiping her appropriately. While in other episodes God is given more respect, or at least acknowledged as being potentially present, Glory provides an entirely different portrait of a god. All of this makes finding a unified take on anything in the show very difficult.[41]

The only overriding worldview in the show is postmodernism, which refuses to make any absolute claims or construct a unified narrative out of the universe. Ultimately, the conclusions drawn by the show are social rather than spiritual. The final season ends with the Scooby Gang casting a spell that changes the entire nature of the universe. Instead of one chosen, divinely ordained Slayer, multiple girls with the potential can become slayers and go out into the word to work and fight against evil. The show is not ultimately about the mythical elements it uses. Rather, these elements are used to explore issues of the real world. And just as the allegorical nature of the show gradually became literal as the seasons progressed—monsters becoming evil humans, vampiric assault becoming attempted rape, supernatural chaos becoming random shootings—the show concludes with the only remaining vampire of any importance (Spike) dying sacrificially and the rest of the characters moving out to shape a new world for themselves.

In *Dracula*, the vampire was used to set up a Christian mission against sin. In Anne Rice's fiction, the vampire was also used for a spiritual purpose—not explicitly a Christian purpose, yet definitely a spiritual one. But with *Buffy* we see a shift. The show explores spiritual and theological themes rooted in the vampire tradition, yet it resists any sort of spiritual affirmation through the way it expresses multiple worldviews at once. In interviews, Joss Whedon has called himself a "hard-line, angry atheist"[42] but claims to believe there is a "religion in narrative."[43] *Buffy* makes this evident. Whatever else *Buffy the Vampire Slayer* was or is, it is an attempt to find value in a world that is no longer spiritual or meaningful.

5

Sookie Stackhouse

Sex and the Socialized Vampire

"You're a Christian," he said, as if he'd discovered I was a hermaphrodite or a fruitarian.

"I'm a real bad one," I said hurriedly.

The fairy Dillon and Sookie in *Dead and Gone*

Sookie Stackhouse, the main character and first-person narrator of Charlaine Harris's Southern Vampire Mysteries, doesn't have anything resembling a normal life. Born a telepath, she has always been able to read other people's thoughts, which has prevented her from developing typical social relationships. Because of this, she considers herself a loner without the possibility of a normal future. She meets her first vampire at Merlotte's, the bar where she's a waitress in rural Louisiana. From that moment on, her life spins off on a different path, where the mythical and supernatural become reality in a way she never imagined. In the latest book, *Dead and Gone*, Sookie reflects on the bizarre nature of her life, where supernatural reality has accumulated to an almost incomprehensible extent:

> I had a moment of disconnect, as if I were standing back from my own life and viewing it from afar. The vampires owed me money and favors for my services to them. The Weres had declared me a friend of the pack for my help during the just-completed war. I was pledged to Eric, which seemed to mean I was engaged or even married. My brother was a werepanther. My great-grandfather was a fairy. It took me a moment to pull myself back into my own skin. My life was too weird.[1]

The first supernatural reality Sookie must confront, however, is the nature of the vampire, and this remains one of Harris's primary interests throughout the series.

Bill, the vampire who walked into Merlotte's and changed Sookie's life, is a Southern gentleman who was made a vampire just after the Civil War. He is Sookie's first entrance into vampire culture. When she overhears the thoughts of a nasty couple—the Rattrays or the "Rats" as she calls them—and realizes they plan to drain Bill's blood and sell it on the black market (since vampire blood, which increases sexual potency and has healing abilities for humans, has become a popular drug in this fictional world), Sookie goes to save him. Thus, Harris's first depiction of a vampire in the series is not the unnatural threatening power of *Dracula* or the handsome, mysterious hero that Angel is in *Buffy*. Rather, our first image is a rather weak one—Bill laid out in a parking lot and imprisoned by silver chains, helpless as his blood is drained and a blond waitress saves him. Vampires in the Southern Vampire Mysteries are humanized in a way they weren't in earlier stories, and one of the ways we see this is in this first encounter. As vampires become a part of human society, they are forced to deal with the social vulnerabilities that are an inevitable part of the human condition.

Although Harris does not ignore the spiritual dimensions of her depiction of vampires, her focus on the social dimensions and her compartmentalizing of religious issues makes her portrayal of the vampire more secular than most earlier vampire books. While Sookie clearly considers herself a Christian, she consistently separates her faith from her understanding of and interaction with vampires. Thus the resulting portrait of the vampire in the books is a secular one. In the HBO series *True Blood*, based on Harris's novels, we see even a further secularization as religion as a whole is called into question through the use of the vampire and other supernatural realities.

The Vampire Disability

From the beginning of the first Sookie Stackhouse novel, *Dead Until Dark*, readers find the premise regarding vampires different from vampire mythology. As in other vampire fiction like Laurell K. Hamilton's Anita Blake, Vampire Hunter series, vampires and other supernatural creatures coexist as part of human culture in Harris's novels. But in the Southern Vampire Mysteries, this is a new development. No longer lurking in the shadows, vampires in Harris's novels have come "out of the coffin," have declared themselves to the world, and have become a legally recognized minority.[2] By understanding vampires in the way contemporary culture understands racial or physical difference, Harris has reenvisioned the place and nature of vampires in her fictional world, placing them in social terms rather than in theological terms.

83

It is their social position that is at issue with this premise, not their theological or spiritual position as damned or not damned, souled or unsouled—as we see in *Dracula*, the Vampire Chronicles, and *Buffy*. Even their distinct characteristics—feeding on blood, without breath or a heartbeat, unable to go out in the sun or tolerate garlic or silver—have been explained away in a socially acceptable way. Sookie, the first-person narrator of the books, explains that, although the "old tales" say that vampires are dead, the "politically correct" and "publicly backed" theory is that vampires have been infected by a virus that makes them seem dead for a couple of days and "thereafter allergic to sunlight, silver, and garlic."[3] The Japanese invention of synthetic blood-substitute has allowed them to reveal themselves to the world, since they no longer have to kill or harm humans in order to feed. In many ways, this premise has entirely removed the figure of the vampire from its theological foundation, posing it only in social terms.

Harris's portrayal of vampires in the novels is not as simplistic as that, however. She certainly uses them to explore social and ethical issues regarding race, difference, and prejudice, but much of the politically correct rhetoric is used tongue in cheek. This is because the underlying assumption about vampires, one Sookie herself gradually comes to realize throughout the first novel, is that vampires are indeed what they have always been understood to be. Friend, boss, and shape-shifter, Sam Merlotte, is the one who convinces Sookie of the supernatural reality of the vampire nature. He says, "I'm sorry, Sookie. But Bill doesn't just have a virus. He's really, really dead."[4] Because the vampire characteristics are not genuinely explained away by a virus, Harris is able to explore some of the same issues that previous vampire stories explored regarding violence, temptation, and guilt. But even as she does so, the social concerns remain paramount for her rather than spiritual ones.

Even though the vampire nature has been socially sanitized with the development of synthetic blood, vampires certainly have not become safe in this fictional world. In Sookie's early reflections about their social situation, readers learn that there remains the possibility of an "Unfortunate Incident"—the vampire "euphemism for the bloody slaying of a human."[5] The fake blood isn't as satisfying to vampires as genuine human blood, as the act of feeding is as important to vampires as the taste and nourishment the blood provides.

Even vampires like Bill, who are trying to "mainstream," are tempted to indulge in what comes more naturally to them. In *Dead Until Dark*, Bill says that because he is a vampire, he doesn't "care about people automatically" the way humans do.[6] He explains to Sookie his history with violence, admitting that, when he was younger, he sometimes killed people by accident when he didn't control himself enough. Back then, he had to hunt to eat, since there was no such thing as artificial blood. However, he adds, "But I had been a good man when I'd been alive—I mean, before I caught the virus. I tried to be civilized about it, select bad people as my victims, never feed on children."[7] While the vampire instinct is always to feed on and thus harm humans, Harris gives her vampires free will. That is, like Bill, they are able to control their instincts and live more like humans.

This ability to control themselves—without gaining a soul as in *Buffy* or by gut-wrenching effort as in Anne Rice's novels—sets them apart from the earlier vampire stories. Being a vampire is almost like living with a disability, a word that is used quite often in the books. It makes it harder for vampires to function as respectable, humane citizens, but not impossible. Their nature does not doom them to sin as the vampires in the stories before them.

That is not to say the spiritual element isn't present at all in Harris's portrayal of vampires. In a conversation between Bill and Sookie in *Dead Until Dark*, the issue of whether vampires have souls comes to the forefront. When Sookie asks him if he agrees with the Catholic Church's belief that vampires have lost their souls, Bill replies, "I have no way of knowing. . . . Personally, I think not. There is something in me that isn't cruel, not murderous, even after all these years. Though I can be both."[8] Sookie immediately absolves him of guilt by saying that it is not his fault if he was infected by a virus, but Bill—and all of the other vampires in the novel—are not given a free pass because of their natures. After Bill almost forces himself on her after a violent encounter in a bar, Sookie manages to stop him from feeding on her when she doesn't want him to. Sookie herself seems to be conflicted about whether this behavior makes him genuinely guilty or not: "He didn't need to apologize. He'd been doing what nature dictated, at least as natural as vampires got. He didn't bother to. I would kind of liked to hear an apology."[9] So the books work with an ongoing tension between absolving vampires from guilt because of their "disability" or holding them accountable when they do something humans understand as wrong. This tension is never resolved completely and so the moral questions and answers remain in the gray area.

One of the distinct features of the books is that Sookie and the other characters continue to try to understand these moral questions—Are vampires wrong to harm humans in order to feed? Is it their fault if it's the only way they can survive?—in social terms rather than spiritual terms. This marks a difference from the earlier stories I have explored. While Sookie sometimes reflects on her own behavior from a spiritual perspective as a Christian, she almost never considers the vampires through the same lens. In *Dead as a Doornail*, Sookie muses,

> Just when I thought I was used to them, vampires would show me their true face, and I would have to remind myself all over again that they were a different race. Or maybe it was the centuries of conditioning that made the difference; decades of disposing of people as they chose, taking what they wanted, enduring the dichotomy of being the most powerful beings on earth in the darkness, and yet completely helpless and vulnerable during the hours of light.[10]

Her rationale here is characteristic of the way the vampires are understood throughout the books. They are not human. While they can choose to function effectively within human society, they will never think or act exactly as humans do. This difference bothers Sookie, but she also has trouble judging them for it. If being a vampire is classified as just another social difference, then the possibility of making moral judgments becomes difficult.

Prejudice and Christian Fanaticism

There are some characters in the books who have no problem making moral judgments against vampires, and that is because they see vampires through a narrow spiritual perspective. Early on in *Dead Until Dark*, readers learn that there are certain "reactionaries" who think that "vampires were damned right off the bat."[11] For the most part, these characters are Christians, although in *Club Dead* we learn that the vampires in the Islamic nations had "fared the worst."[12] It seems to be characters who understand vampires through the narrow lens of religion who end up being the fanatics

87

who want to wipe vampires from the face of the earth. In *Definitely Dead*, Sookie explains, "The churches of America hadn't come to grips with the reality of vampires. To call their policies confused was putting it mildly."[13] She goes on to explain that the Catholic Church was holding a convocation to decide whether vampires are irrevocably damned, and the Episcopal Church had voted that vampires could take communion but couldn't become priests. It is much more difficult to understand vampires religiously than it is socially because it comes down to issues of the soul.

The Fellowship of the Sun is a fanatical religious group that takes all of the complexity out of a spiritual understanding of vampires. The Fellowship is a consistent feature of the books, starting with the second book, *Living Dead in Dallas*, when the Fellowship is a key player in the plot. The Fellowship is the main example of Christian fanaticism—radical humans who are antivampire for religious reasons. They try to lobby for political support in their antivampire crusade and also resort to acts of domestic terrorism to prove their point or sway their opponents.

All of the Fellowship's actions are done in the name of religion. In *Living Dead*, Sookie's encounters with the Fellowship lead her to understand that all of its members see themselves not as a social or political group, but as a church.[14] She describes a sign on the lawn of the Fellowship center that reads, "FELLOWSHIP OF THE SUN CENTER—ONLY JESUS ROSE FROM THE DEAD." Sookie, who has clearly gone to Sunday school, argues that Lazarus too rose from the dead: "Jerks can't even get their scripture right."[15] So Harris makes it clear that the Fellowship is not representative of all Christians or all religious characters. They are portrayed negatively because they are extremists and hypocrites who use religion to pursue their own intolerant agenda.

Vampires themselves are not immune to seeing themselves spiritually, as Godfrey in *Living Dead in Dallas* proves. But, like the Fellowship, Godfrey's narrow religious lens has led him to poor judgment, since he has betrayed his fellow vampires to the Fellowship and puts others at risk in his own pursuit of salvation. Godfrey, overwhelmed with his own guilt, wants to commit suicide, to "meet the sun" for religious reasons. He tells Sookie, "Tomorrow I atone for my sin publicly. . . . Tomorrow I greet the dawn. For the first time in a thousand years, I will see the sun. Then I will see the face of God."[16] Godfrey feeds on children, so—as sex and feeding for vampires in the books are almost indistinguishable—he is basically a pedophile.

Because of Godfrey's proclivities, Sookie does not dispute the fact that ending his existence might be a good choice. But she naturally objects to the idea that she would be drawn into his act of redemption against her will by being killed with him. Steve Newlin, the leader of the Fellowship—resenting her interference, her relationship with vampires, and her own "unnatural" abilities—wants to tie her to Godfrey and burn her with him as a religious ritual. She challenges this idea with Godfrey, claiming that most people will never genuinely believe killing a woman like that to be a religious ceremony. She does not appear to be wrong in this. Harris never universalizes all religious people as fanatics. Sookie tells Godfrey to pursue his atonement, to meet the sun, privately, adding "God'll be watching, I promise you. That's who you should care about."[17] Sookie, who went to church and took Communion the week before, has a religious perspective that is not fanatical. But her perspective also compartmentalizes religion to a certain extent. She is able to separate her religious beliefs from her reflections about who and what vampires are, and thus appreciate vampires socially as well as spiritually.

Blood and Sex

Just like Anne Rice's and later Stephenie Meyer's vampires, Charlaine Harris's vampires are, for the most part, beautiful and desirable. They are pale, of course, because they cannot be out in the sunlight. While they have distinct features and characteristics of the time and place they were turned (for instance, Godfrey has primitive tattoos and Bill has nineteenth-century sideburns), they are consistently attractive to people of both sexes and have a clearly sexual appeal. As in *Buffy*, they change physically when they are about to feed. But while the whole face of *Buffy*'s vampires alter, Harris's vampires merely extend their fangs. The extension of the fangs is used as a physical sign of lust—either bloodlust or sexual lust. There is consistently an overlap in the way Harris imposes these two lusts on her vampires. This is because, in the Southern Vampire Mysteries, the vampire's desire to feed and desire to have sex are impossible to separate.

A significant part of vampire culture in the books is its overt sexuality. Sookie faces this from the very beginning when, after she saves him, Bill comes on to her with a comment about the "juicy artery in your groin." Although he is ostensibly talking about drinking her blood, she correctly understands the comment as sexual and tartly tells him not to "talk dirty."[18] When Sookie goes with Bill to Fangtasia, the vampire bar owned by Eric, the vampire sheriff of Bill's area, she notices that all anyone is thinking about in the bar is sex. It is full of "Fangbangers," humans who get sexual thrill out of being bitten by vampires. And over and over again as the books progress and Sookie has more experiences with various vampires, she recognizes that, for vampires, the act of feeding is indistinguishable from the act of sex. In *Living Dead in Dallas*, she reflects, "Sex and food were so tied together in the vampire life system that I couldn't imagine a vampire having sex with someone nonhuman, that is, someone he couldn't get blood from."[19] Both acts of penetration offer vampires the same kind of satisfaction.

Even vampires who are trying to mainstream and exist only on synthetic blood are still tempted to feed on humans. This temptation to feed is always described in sexual terms, like when Bill is tempted in *Dead Until Dark* by his three vampire visitors to feed on the human lover of one of them. The overlap between sex and drinking blood is part of the overwhelming nature of Sookie's introduction to what being a vampire means. In that scene, she is bombarded by both the overt sexuality and the visceral power of Bill's desire to drink human blood. Afterward, Bill tells her, "Sookie, our life is seducing and taking and has been for centuries. Synthetic blood and grudging human acceptance isn't going to change that overnight—or over a decade."[20] This conflation of sex and feeding is a central part of the vampire nature in Harris's books. It certainly is not original with her. We have seen the act of drinking blood eroticized in each of the previous chapters. But Harris socializes it and highlights the sex act itself rather than simply making the act of feeding erotic.[21]

Because vampire blood has qualities that heal, strengthen, and intoxicate humans, the act of drinking blood in Harris's novels works both ways—that is, the human can drink from the vampire as much as the vampire can drink from the human. It is sexualized both ways. While Bill bites Sookie and drinks her blood nearly every time they have sex, the times she drinks from him are also sexualized. In *Dead Until Dark*, she needs to drink Bill's blood in order to have enough strength to carry on, but Bill makes the necessary act of her drinking his blood into sex:

> "Drink," he said raggedly, and I sucked hard. He groaned, louder, deeper, and I felt him pressing against me. A little

ripple of madness went through me, and I attached myself to him like a barnacle, and he entered me, began moving, his hands now gripping my hip bones. I drank and saw visions, visions all with a background of darkness, of white things coming up from the ground and going hunting, the thrill of the run through the woods, the prey panting ahead and the excitement of its fear; pursuit, legs pumping, hearing the thrumming of blood through the veins of the pursued . . .

Bill made a noise deep in his chest and convulsed inside me. I raised my head from his neck, and a wave of dark delight carried me out to sea.

This was pretty exotic stuff for a telepathic barmaid from northern Louisiana.[22]

Similarly, the more Sookie drinks of vampire bar-owner Eric's blood, the more she is unwillingly tied to him. This means they can feel each other's presence and sense what the other is thinking. But one of the additional consequences is a more heightened desire for him, and in the later novels this fact causes Sookie a lot of emotional confusion, as she has trouble deciding whether she is genuinely attracted and drawn to Eric or if it is just the connection of their blood.

In *Dracula*, the eroticizing of the vampire act of feeding is always connected to the temptation into sin—thus it was used for spiritual purposes. While Rice and *Buffy* both highlight the erotic aspect of the vampire experience more than Stoker and spend some time emphasizing the sexual aspects in a positive sense, in those examples the eroticism is still tied—at least in part—to temptation and thus used to develop the theme of sin. This is not the case for Harris's novel. Certainly there is sexual temptation, but it is not used for the purposes of establishing a spiritual theme of sin. Rather, Harris puts it in a social context, to graphically explore romantic relationships between characters and to examine how overt sexuality distinguishes vampire culture from human (particularly Southern) culture, where sexuality is repressed or made private. Aside from a few passing comments about how God might have a problem with her jumping into bed with an assortment of men, Sookie's experiences with sexualized vampire acts have very few spiritual implications.

Faith and Morality

Sookie is explicitly a Christian in the books. She calls herself a Christian and her personal faith does have certain implications on her life and behavior. While it certainly does not stop her from having sex outside of marriage, she does use her understanding of Christianity to try to make sense of her life. She goes to church regularly. In *Living Dead in Dallas*, she tells Godfrey that she went to church in the last week or two, although she admits in *From Dead to Worse* that she doesn't always listen to the sermon but rather uses the time to think.[23] In *Dead Until Dark*, Sid Matt gives Sookie some advice about her gift of telepathy, which she has always seen as a disability: "I'm sure the Good Lord gave you this problem I've heard about for a reason. You have to learn how to use it for his glory." While it is not clear whether this statement is supposed to be a narrative truth, Sookie is struck by it and vows to "chew over" it.[24] Sookie believes in God and wants to live as a good Christian, but as her world changes with her increasing interaction with supernatural creatures, she comes to see that her Christian worldview simply is not large enough to cover what her life has become.

Harris's emphasis on Christianity, at least as Sookie understands it, is in the concepts of mercy and turning the other cheek, and this is clearly opposed to the Christian fanaticism

93

we see in the Fellowship of the Sun. Sookie is constantly torn by moral issues regarding the taking of human life, right from the beginning of *Dead Until Dark* when Bill kills the Rattrays after they have tried to drain him. She expresses her confusion over recognizing murder and yet not feeling as opposed to it as she should: "I couldn't regret that the world was rid of the Rats. But I had to look this straight in the face. I couldn't dodge the realization that I was sitting in the lap of a murderer. Yet I was quite happy to sit there, his arms around me."[25] Although she is able to justify certain acts of murder that Bill commits, like the Rattrays and her uncle who molested her as a child, she still recognizes a moral conflict there and does not immediately gloss over all of the more morally ambiguous aspects of being a vampire the way we will see Bella do in the Twilight saga. In *Dead Until Dark*, Harris sets up a pattern of Sookie pulling back from her relationship with Bill whenever she's confronted with these moral conflicts. She tells Bill that she loves him but that "I have to live here and I have to live with myself."[26] So she has to figure out whether a relationship with a vampire is worth all the moral and emotional struggles it must entail.

Not only does Sookie have to come to terms with the moral questions surrounding the nature of a vampire, she has to come to terms with the morality of acts that she herself commits. In *Club Dead*, she kills the vampire Lorena, who was torturing Bill. Although the killing is easily justifiable as self-defense, and Lorena falls on a stake so Sookie does not have to consider herself directly responsible for it, Sookie still feels horrible about the death.

In the next book, *Dead to the World*, Sookie has to kill Debbie, the shape-shifter who has tried to kill her more than once. This act of killing someone who is mostly human is one that Sookie keeps coming back to with guilt and regret, despite the fact that it too is self-defense. Sookie's guilt is directly tied to her Christian faith. As she processes it in a discussion with Eric, who participated in the killing, Eric admits that he cannot see it as a wrong. He says, "I was never a Christian. . . . But I can't imagine a belief system that would tell you to sit still and get slaughtered." Sookie reflects in response, "I blinked, wondering if that wasn't exactly what Christianity taught. But I am no theologian or Bible scholar, and I would have to leave the judgment on my action to God, who was also no theologian."[27] The question seems to revolve here on the idea of turning the other cheek, which Sookie is convinced Christianity would have had her do—despite the fact that Debbie had just shot at her and would have killed her had Eric not jumped in front of the bullet instead.

In *Dead and Gone*, she has similar religious reflections— this time prompted by her admission that she can no longer support her brother, Jason, in every situation in his life, after he has forced her into the situation of smashing a brick on the hand of a good man and breaking his fingers. She believes turning her back on her brother because of this makes her a "bad Christian," and she wonders if "crisis moments in my life hadn't come down to two choices: be a bad Christian or die. I'd chosen life every time."[28] This is the same moral conflict that Sookie faces throughout the books—trying to reconcile what life requires of her in terms of acts of violence or ruthlessness with her understanding of Christian teachings about forgiveness and mercy. She goes on to reflect,

> Would the people I was serving laugh, if they knew what I was thinking? Would my anxiety over the state of my soul amuse them? Lots of them would probably tell me that all situations are covered in the Bible, and that if I read the Book more, I'd find my answers there.
>
> That hadn't worked for me so far, but I wasn't giving up.[29]

Sookie never comes up with any answers, and her place in the world—halfway between human society and supernatural society—forces her over and over again to defy her religious beliefs in order to survive. She must compartmentalize her spiritual faith if she wants to go on living.

This same conflict comes up again in *Dead and Gone* when she kills a fairy who was about to kill her. She cannot rejoice about it as Dillon, also a fairy, says she should. When she hesitates about being glad that she killed the other fairy, he accuses her of being a Christian, as horrified as if she were a "hermaphrodite or fruitarian."[30] But the fact that the fairy understands Christianity in the same way as Sookie makes it clear that this conflict is an overriding theme in the books and not just a feature of Sookie's misunderstanding of the gospel. Harris uses this conflict throughout, but she also has Sookie continually forced to push aside the religious issues. They bother her, but she can never act on them—or she would be killed. And that is not something she is willing to let happen.

Sookie's ultimate worldview regarding morality and the supernatural world seems to be summed up in one of her discussions with Sam in *From Dead to Worse*. She tells him, "People aren't better or worse than the supernaturals, but they're not all there is, either."[31] Narrow human morality and worldview simply is not large enough to encompass a world that includes vampires, werewolves, shape-shifters, witches, fairies, and who knows what other supernatural beings. While Sookie wants to hold onto her religious and moral understandings, they just cannot be consistently sustained in a world so large. While she has not yet figured out a worldview that will encompass them, the best answer seems to be understanding and flexibility—social virtues—rather than spiritual virtues like faith and morality.

True Blood

The HBO series *True Blood* is based on Harris's Southern Vampire Mysteries. In many ways, it stays true to the books—using most of the same characters and characterizations and a number of the same plot elements. Like the books, it emphasizes the sexual nature of the vampire acts and the social implications of their coming "out of the coffin" and becoming part of mainstream society. It also sustains Sookie's character as a Christian who faces worldview conflicts as her belief system is stretched to the breaking point. The television series adds themes that Harris does not spend much time exploring—particularly that of addiction, as we see in the story lines of Tara's mother's alcoholism and Jason and Amy's addiction to vampire blood (V-juice) in the first season. But more than in the book series, the television series questions the fundamental nature of religion and belief—particularly in the second season—and so the show is more purely secular than the book series.

On the surface, the series does not appear secular. In fact, the opening credits, set to Jace Everett's country song "Bad Things," juxtaposes sexual, grotesque, and religious images quite blatantly. Paired with scenes of a woman in sexy lingerie, a couple having sex on a pool table, and pole dancing are religious scenes of church people praying, singing in a choir, being moved by the Spirit, and being baptized in a river. While Harris certainly conflates sex and vampire culture, she never conflates religion and sex. And that is what the juxtaposition of these opposing images imply in the opening credits of *True Blood*—that there is a relationship between being moved by God and being moved by lust, being overcome with religious fervor and being overcome with sexual desire. Intermingled with these scenes are grotesque images like a snake about to strike and a dead, bloody rat and one ironic

97

image of a marquee sign saying "God hates fangs." With the repeated refrain of the song "I Want to Do Bad Things with You," the opening credits seem to be questioning the validity of religious experience—or at least the distinctness of religious experience—and this idea is carried through in the plot, particularly in the second season.

In the first season, built around the plot of *Dead Until Dark*, which explores the search for the serial murderer of female fangbangers, religious issues are considered only in minor ways. But from the first episode, "Strange Love," Sookie (Anna Paquin) is set up as a good southern Christian, chiding Tara (Rutina Wesley) for using the "J word" (taking Jesus's name in vain) and telling Lafayette (Nelsan Ellis) he shouldn't speak "nasty talk" in front of her.[32] In "The First Taste," the second episode, after hearing a news report in which the Fellowship of the Sun uses Christianity to pursue an antivampire agenda, Sookie innocently tells her grandmother, "I don't think Jesus would mind if somebody was a vampire."[33] And, in "Mine," her grandmother is the one who voices Sid Matt's piece of advice from the books, when she tells Sookie that there is a "purpose for everything that God creates," including vampires and Sookie's gift of telepathy, and God will "reveal that purpose when the time is right."[34] In the next episode, "Escape from Dragon House," Sookie corrects Sam (Sam Trammell) after they find the body of a murdered girl, telling him sharply that "God didn't do this."[35] Sookie is set up as a Christian as she is in the books, and her gentle, innocent brand of Christianity intentionally contrasts with the narrow, hypocritical, and fanatical religion of the Fellowship of the Sun as depicted in the show.

In the first season, there are also some additional plot elements that add to the portrayal of religion. In "Sparks Fly Out," there is an amusing scene when Hoyt and his mother unsuccessfully try to hide the cross in the church before Bill (Stephen Moyer) comes to speak to the Descendants of the Glorious Dead about his experiences in the Civil War. When the cross is unmovable, they end up hiding it with the American flag. Bill removes it, obviously unaffected by the cross despite vampire mythology to the contrary.

In the first season, there is also a plotline about Tara and her mother. Her alcoholic, abusive mother talks the talk of a Christian, even as she wallows in destructive behavior. Then she goes through an exorcism ritual to rid herself of the demon that makes her drink—a ritual that is more in line with voodoo and African animistic religion than with Christianity. When the ritual seems to be successful, Tara decides to go through one too, in hopes it will help her pull together her life. But she later finds out Miss Jeanette is not a religious authority but rather a fraud and con artist. Both of these examples imply a light skepticism toward Christianity—while part of Southern culture, it doesn't have any particular power universally or individually.

While season 1 points here and there to a skepticism about religion, this is more fully developed in season 2, whose central theme, as *True Blood* creator Alan Ball says, is "the power of belief."[36] The two major plot arcs involve Sookie, Eric, and the others' infiltration of the Fellowship of the Sun to find the kidnapped vampire Godric and the carnal devolution of the town of Bon Temps under the maenad Maryann's bacchanal influence. Both of these plot arcs center on the idea of faith or belief, and ultimately both are destructive. The Christian fanaticism of the Fellowship is shown to be both hypocritical and destructive. And it is also shown to be no less carnal and intoxicating than Maryann's pulling the citizens of Bon Temps under her supernatural influence and causing them to explode into sexual orgies and violence. The scenes at the Fellowship's leadership conference—including the brilliantly ironic, sexed-up abstinence song, "Jesus Asked Me Out Today," sung by a Britney-type pop singer in pigtails—are paralleled to the Bon Temps orgy scenes in the way those under its influence are drawn mindlessly into empty fervor and carnality. Thus the Christianity of the Fellowship is shown as equal to the bacchanal religion that Maryann is forcing on citizens of Bon Temps. While Harris clearly distinguishes between the radicals at the Fellowship and Christians like Sookie, the television series blurs those lines until it questions religion as a whole.

In the first episode of the second season, "Nothing But the Blood," the maenad Maryann (Michelle Forbes) says, "The Greeks knew there is the flimsiest veil between us and the divine. They didn't see the gods as being inaccessible, the way everyone does today."[37] This sets the stage for the chaos she brings about in Bon Temps. By infecting everyone with extremes of emotion and desire, Maryann is trying to reach what is later referred to as "The God Who Comes" (double entendre certainly intended). But as the vampire Queen of Louisiana, Sophie-Anne, tells Bill in the penultimate episode of the season, the problem is that maenads like Maryann are waiting for a god who never actually comes: "Gods never actually show up. They only exist in humans' minds, like money and morality."[38] And thus the key to defeating Maryann is to fake her into believing a god has actually appeared. Like the Fellowship, Maryann's belief seems to be based on an insupportable foundation, a god that doesn't actually exist or at least never exerts his presence in human experience.

The moment in the second season where a spiritual reality seems genuine is when Godric (Allan Hyde) meets the sun. As in *Living Dead in Dallas*, Godric (who was called Godfrey in the book) lets himself get taken by the Fellowship because he was ready to end his life as a vampire. In the book, this is prompted by guilt. In *True Blood*, it seems to be more exhaustion than guilt. Godric is simply tired of living and can't see anything constructive coming out of existence or society anymore. He does speak of an act of "atonement," but the guilt that led up to this need for atonement isn't clear the way his pedophile tendencies make it clear in the book. Instead, he seems to be taking on himself the weight of society's guilt—human and vampire, their inability to live in peace with one another the way he tells Steve Newlin he thinks is possible. Thus he becomes almost a Christ figure, which he isn't in the book.

In the episode "I Will Rise Up," Eric (Alexander Skarsgård) begs Godric not to destroy himself and then offers to stay with him at the end, a gesture that would kill Eric as well; but Godric refuses and Sookie stays with him instead, in Eric's place. Sookie is moved by Godric's and perhaps by Eric's grief—as she has (unwillingly) drunk his blood and now has an emotional connection to him—and she cries when she tells Godric she understands. Godric asks her if she believes in God, which she tells him she does. Then he asks if she thinks God will punish him for his sins, and Sookie answers with her particular slant on Christianity, "God doesn't punish. God forgives." But it is not spiritual forgiveness that seems to matter to Godric at the end. When he sees Sookie crying, he says, "A human with me at the end, and human tears. Two thousand years, and I can still be surprised. In this, I see God."[39] It is in the human connection that Godric finds a meaningful understanding of religious experience—not in any spiritual truths. And this seems to be as close to a conclusion as the show reaches on the issue. It is not in religion but in human society, human feeling, that we can reach something that feels like God.

101

Season 3 of *True Blood* continues to explore the social themes of the earlier seasons, growing ever extreme in its portrait of sexuality, violence, politics, and relationships. In both *True Blood* and the Southern Vampire Mysteries, the figure of the vampire has become mostly secular, used to explore social themes like human difference, sexuality, and tolerance rather than spiritual themes like sin, temptation, and redemption. The only redemption that seems necessary or possible is a society—both human and supernatural—at peace with one another. And the way the creators seem to feel this should happen is through human understanding on an individual level. While religion is still at issue in these stories, the vampire itself no longer has genuine theological significance.

6

Stephenie Meyer's Twilight Saga

The Vampire as Teenage Heartthrob

It's not what you *are*, stupid, it's what you *do*!

Bella to Jacob in *New Moon*

The cover of Stephenie Meyer's novel *Twilight* displays the striking image of a red apple being offered in two pale, cupped hands. The symbolic significance of this image is rich, especially when combined with the book's epigraph, taken from Genesis 2:17: "But of the tree of the knowledge of good and evil, thou shalt not eat of it: for in the day that thou eatest thereof thou shalt surely die." These early indicators set up the novel and those that follow in the series as having the potential for the spiritual and theological reflection that has been a part of the vampire tradition since Stoker's *Dracula*. But that potential is never capitalized on in the novels. Any reference to religion is passing, and any opportunity to use

103

the spiritual themes available in the figure of the vampire are ignored in favor of a characterization of vampires that turns them into little more than glorified humans or generic superheroes. In Meyer's Twilight Saga, we can see the end result of the process of secularization. Although Meyer herself is a Mormon, spirituality and religion are not genuinely explored in the books.[1] Stripped of theological significance, the vampire has become instead an ideal romantic alpha-hero.

While religion is not completely absent in the books of the Twilight Saga, it certainly is not a dominant interest as it is in earlier vampire books by Stoker and Rice or in the television show *Buffy the Vampire Slayer*. The whole philosophy of "vegetarian" vampires—vampires who choose to not feed on humans but instead exist on animal blood—is set up in a pseudoreligious context. Carlisle's father was a seventeenth-century preacher who participated in fanatical religious persecution of supernatural creatures like witches, werewolves, and vampires, and it was in a raid on a coven of vampires that Carlisle himself was attacked and turned. He had to flee because he knew his father would not have mercy on anyone—even his own son—infected by the vampire venom. After trying unsuccessfully to kill himself, Carlisle realized he could survive on animal blood and decided to attempt a new kind of life as a vampire—a vampire that does no harm.

Aside from the Native American characters' belief in spirits, Carlisle is the only character in the novels who espouses a clear religious faith. In *New Moon*, he tells Bella, "So I didn't agree with my father's particular brand of faith. But, never, in the nearly four hundred years now since I was born, have I ever seen anything to make me doubt whether God exists in some form or other. Not even the reflection in the mirror."[2] But despite his background and this statement, he is not a particularly religious character. Certainly none of the others are either. Edward has fears about Bella's losing her soul in *New Moon*, but these fears are either eliminated or forgotten by the end of the book, and never become a central issue again. The focus of the books is secular, so much so that the figure of the vampire itself becomes secular and is used primarily to explore themes of romantic love and family. In my analysis of the Twilight Saga, I will explore how Meyer portrays vampires and how free will—the ability to choose to be good—replaces the vampire's evil nature from traditional vampire stories. Then I will consider how the idealized vampire becomes a romantic hero of fantasy, and thus romantic love is posed as the ultimate human experience in the novels.

More Angel Than Man

On beginning *Twilight*, it soon becomes obvious that Meyer's portrayal of vampires is not the traditional one. As has now become common, each new vampire story defines the nature of vampires in its own distinct way, setting itself apart from others while establishing itself within a particular line of tradition. Like Anne Rice's vampires, Meyer's are striking in their physical beauty. Their skin is pale—a constant for vampires—but she makes a point of the shifting color of their eyes, the color reflecting when and how they have last fed. They move gracefully, like runway models, Bella thinks. And they have dark circles under their eyes, another distinguishing characteristic. When she first sees the Cullens at school, Bella says, "I stared because their faces, so different, so similar, were all devastatingly, inhumanly beautiful."[3] While physically they fit in with a certain vampire tradition, they do not fall in line in a number of other ways.

In the Twilight Saga, vampires are not afraid of the sun. They can go out during the day, making it possible for them to go to high school and function like normal people. Their choice of location is important, however, since they cannot be seen in direct sunlight. This is not because the sun will destroy them—they are not creatures of night or darkness the way traditional vampires are—but because sunlight shows them for what they really are: something more than human. When Bella first sees Edward in the sun, she describes him this way:

> Edward in the sunlight was shocking. I couldn't get used to it, though I'd been staring at him all afternoon. His skin, white despite the faint flush from yesterday's hunting trip, literally sparkled, like thousands of tiny diamonds were embedded in the surface. He lay perfectly still in the grass, his shirt open over his sculpted, incandescent chest, his scintillating arms bare. His glistening, pale lavender lids were shut, though of course he didn't sleep. A perfect statue, carved in some unknown stone, smooth like marble, glittering like crystal.[4]

Vampire skin shines and glistens in the sun, a phenomenon that causes Bella to consistently compare Edward to diamond, sculpture, marble, and crystal. As I'll discuss later, these comparisons have the potential to emasculate Edward, but they also associate him with something higher than human. Bella calls him an angel repeatedly throughout the books, and it is clear—at least physically—why she sees him as such. He is more beautiful, more splendid, more glistening than any human being. Instead of vampirism being an irrevocable damnation, or even a disease or disability to be dealt with, as in Harris's books, Meyer portrays the nature of the vampire as the ideal—as something higher than human, rather than lower.

This higher nature is also evidenced in the vampires' invulnerability. They are faster, stronger, more stealthy, and more powerful than any human being. Their skin is nearly impenetrable, and it is nearly impossible to kill them. While Anne Rice's vampires are difficult to kill, it is only the ancient vampires that really defy destruction (who don't die even when they go out in the sun). But even newborn vampires in the Twilight books can only be killed by tearing them apart and burning the pieces. They are not afraid of religious objects—the Cullens have a cross in their home that was made by Carlisle's father. They cannot be killed with a stake to the heart or a silver bullet. And they do not sleep in coffins. In fact, they do not sleep at all.

In addition, each vampire in the books is idealized and portrayed as something higher than human by possessing some sort of unique gift. Rice's vampires also had gifts—some could read the thoughts of other vampires, some could levitate or move in remarkable ways—but in Rice's novels, those gifts were usually connected to whoever sired them. In the Twilight Saga, each vampire seems to have his or her distinct gift, something that highlights their individuality. Edward tells Bella that each vampire brings with them their strongest characteristic when they are changed.

In *Twilight*, we only see a couple of vampires with distinct abilities. Alice has visions of the future. Edward can read thoughts. By the time we reach the end of *Breaking Dawn* and the Cullens are putting together a force to face down the Volturi, however, these unique gifts or powers have become a much more significant feature of the vampire nature. Zafrina can affect the vision of others. Kate has electric pulses on her skin. Bella learns she herself has the power of a mental shield. While there are some vampires—like Rosalie and Emmett—who are never clearly distinguished by a gift like this, Meyer does eventually make these gifts part of her vampire canon. This additional characteristic makes her vampires more like superheroes than they initially seem.

In nearly every way, Meyer's portrait of the vampire is a vast departure from early portrayals in novels like *Dracula*. Her vampires are not monsters. They are closer to angels or superheroes than they are to demons. And while they thirst for human blood—the consistent characteristic that always defines the vampire nature—they do not deal with the other vulnerabilities that have traditionally been associated with vampires. Many of these characteristics associated the vampire with theology and spirituality, so the lack of them in the Twilight Saga is one way we see the secularization. They are secularized in deeper ways than that, however, as we will see in the remainder of this chapter.

Free Will

More than in the other vampire stories I have explored, Meyer's vampires are capable of free will. For Dracula, free will is not even an option, and *Buffy*'s vampires are only capable of free will when the demon inside of them is countered by a human soul. Rice's vampires have more capacity to freely choose to do good—as Lestat does at the end of *Blood Canticle* in his choice of sacrificial love—but their vampire natures always draw them back into darkness, into torment. This is not true of the *Twilight* vampires. The Cullens, beginning with Carlisle, have made a free choice to be "vegetarian." While it is often a difficult choice to carry out, nothing in their nature prevents them from freely making that choice. Thus, by their choices, they are transformed from being monsters. As Bella tells Jacob in *New Moon* about his being a werewolf, "It's not what you *are*, stupid, it's what you *do*!"[5] Meyer's vampires are defined by their actions rather than by their natures—which dramatically shifts the theological themes inherent in the figure of the vampire. Early on in *Twilight*, when Bella searches the Internet for information on vampires, she sees one reference that gives her hope: "Stregoni benefici: An Italian vampire, said to be on the side of goodness, and a mortal enemy of all evil vampires."[6] It is possible in Meyer's depiction to be a "good" vampire.

The most important choice for vampires in the Twilight Saga is whether to feed on humans or not, whether to be a killer or not. Their instinct is always to drink human blood. It is a physical need, and it is clear that only human blood can fully satisfy them. Carlisle's early experiences set the stage for the rest of the Cullens. When he first became a vampire, he was so "repelled by himself" that he tried to kill himself through starvation. When he realized he could live off of animals instead, he was able to choose to do something other than his hunger dictated: "Over the next months his new philosophy was born. He could exist without being a demon. He found himself again."[7] While this choice prevents the vampires from being fully physically sated, it allows them to participate in more human activities like family and human bonding. This correlation—between choosing not to kill humans and being capable of richer emotional experiences—becomes particularly clear in *Breaking Dawn*, when the Cullens are juxtaposed with the Volturi, who behave as typical vampires and thus do not make those kinds of bonds.

One of Edward's tensions is between his human feelings and his suspicions of his vampire nature. More than the other vampires, he believes himself to be bad at the same time he wants desperately to be good. This guilt and torment is characteristic of vampire stories and is explored in great depth by both Anne Rice and *Buffy the Vampire Slayer*. Its depiction in *Twilight* is fairly simplistic. Edward is indeed troubled by the fact that he is dangerous and that he has the potential to be evil. When Bella acknowledges in *Twilight* that Edward can be dangerous, she adds "But not bad. . . . No, I don't believe that you're bad." Edward's response is, "You're wrong."[8] And Edward certainly struggles whenever he is close to Bella with his desire to feed on her. It is the central conflict in the first book—he loves her but also wants to drink her blood.

Edward's desire, however, is one he can control. He does so by distancing himself physically from her, and in *New Moon* he actually leaves, out of what he believes to be Bella's best interest. But the tension is not an eternal struggle as it was for Lestat or Louis in the Vampire Chronicles, and it does not have to be resolved through painful sacrifice as for Angel or Spike in *Buffy the Vampire Slayer*. In *Breaking Dawn*, Bella becomes a vampire herself and thus Edward's tension is completely resolved. The conflict was not really part of Edward's nature as much as a result of a very particular circumstance—his falling in love with a human. We see little of that tension in the other Cullens, although we are always supposed to believe that the struggle against their vampire thirst is a difficult one. Even so, their thirst is something that can always be overcome, as vampires are as capable of free will as humans are.

Because of this capacity for free will, the vampire existence is not a dark or an especially difficult one—as it has traditionally been portrayed. When Bella and Edward come to their "impasse" at the end of *New Moon*—Bella wanting to become a vampire and Edward resisting it because he believes it would take away her soul—Bella sees very few negative consequences to such a step: "I couldn't really see Edward's point, to be honest. What was so great about mortality? Being a vampire didn't look like such a terrible thing—not the way the Cullens did it, anyway."[9] They are affluent, live in community, and are capable of enjoying human experiences like love and family. Even in their hunting, they are ethically upright. Edward explains to Bella that they take care of the environment and focus in their hunting on areas of overpopulated predators, instead of depleting the animal population through their feeding. While readers are given a few glimpses of remaining tensions, like the scene in *New Moon* when Bella cuts her arms and Jasper can't resist attacking her, Bella seems to approach these as minor inconveniences rather than a profound statement on what it means to be a vampire.

Consistent in all four novels of the Twilight Saga is a belief in free will overcoming anything in one's nature. In *New Moon*, when Bella tries to defend Edward against his own accusations by claiming that what happened to him wasn't his fault, Edward's response is simple and reflects a very similar line from Tolkien's Lord of the Rings: "Like everything in life, I just had to decide what to do with what I was given."[10] A few pages later, Carlisle expresses a similar sentiment, distinguishing his vampire experience from cultural understanding. He says to Bella, "But I'm hoping that there is still a point to this life, even for us. . . . By all accounts, we're damned regardless. But I hope, maybe foolishly, that we'll get some measure of credit for trying."[11] The books seem to affirm that his hope is justified. While they speak occasionally about being "damned" for being what they are, nothing in the novels supports this as a genuine reality, the way it is in Rice's Vampire Chronicles and *Buffy*.

When Bella herself becomes a vampire, the issue of free will is exemplified even more clearly. As soon as she falls in love with Edward, she makes the choice to become a vampire herself. This is a choice the other vampires were not given. She weighs the options and sees an eternity with Edward as a priority over the experiences she would have as a human and her connections to her human family and friends. Even, in *Eclipse*, as she is considering the difficulties of being a vampire, she believes she can handle the bloodthirsty part of her nature as a newborn vampire because she trusts that Edward would keep her from doing anything she doesn't want to do. She never doubts her capacity to keep from hurting anyone, even after she has become a vampire. In *Breaking Dawn*, she actually engages in the foundational vampire experience—drinking blood—before she even becomes a vampire. Because she is pregnant with a half-vampire child, her body needs the blood and she enjoys drinking it—even as a human. She chooses the existence and the nature of a vampire freely and without restraint, and this free will is evident after she is transformed. She doesn't struggle nearly as much as the others do with the desire to feed on humans.

Without the evil, selfish vampire nature as a dominant force in the figure of the vampire, themes like sin and guilt become less powerful or prevalent. Themes of choosing well and doing good are prioritized because the primary vampires in the Twilight novels are constantly making good choices. This is another way the figure of the vampire loses its spiritual or theological significance. Because the power of exercising free will and choosing to do what is right is an ethical question and one that can be explored in purely human, social ways, it doesn't necessarily lead to spiritual reflection the way the sinful vampire nature in the earlier stories consistently did.

Romance: Having It Both Ways

Instead of using the vampire to represent theological or philosophical questions, Meyer uses the vampire as a convenient alpha-hero. As in Harris's novels, the vampire is invested with heights of attractiveness and desirability. But, unlike in the Sookie Stackhouse books, these traits are not paired with less desirable traits that raise plausible and compelling tensions within the vampire-human relationship. While certain tensions are certainly addressed, they are summarily resolved in a way that shapes an adolescent female fantasy of a romantic love without any real responsibility or consequences. Bella is consistently able to "have it both ways."

Bella is set up at the beginning of *Twilight* as somewhat representative of the typical teenage girl—that is, she feels plain, clumsy, and uninteresting. She also, as is common for most people her age, feels isolated and almost alien. She says, "Sometimes I wondered if I was seeing the same things through my eyes that the rest of the world was seeing through theirs. Maybe there was a glitch in my brain."[12] While she sees herself as distinct and atypical, this very characteristic makes her easily relatable for most readers. It is essential in romance novels—if not every kind of relationship-oriented fiction—for the reader to identify with the main character. This isolation of Bella's is an important step in that process, as it calls on the (ironically) common human experience, often heightened in adolescence, of feeling alone and different.

Bella immediately feels a kinship with the Cullens, whom she does not yet know are vampires, because she understands that they too are "outsiders, clearly not accepted."[13] It is from this point of social alienation that Bella begins the process of finding community and romantic love. But instead of doing so in a "natural" way, Bella's social and sexual maturation are found in the realm of the supernatural. As such, she lives out a typical female fantasy of being loved in a way that seems thrilling and, at the same time, without any real responsibility—because she pours herself into Edward.

The first steps of Edward and Bella's relationship fit the pattern of traditional romantic fiction. On first sight, they are attracted to each other—Bella overwhelmed by his physical beauty and mystery and Edward revealing an obsession with her that is not immediately understood. When Bella first makes physical contact with him, she feels the clichéd "electric current,"[14] although it is not clear whether the sensation is literal or emotional, since the story has supernatural elements. Like every good romantic hero, Edward is unknowable, with depths that both draw and scare Bella. His initial behavior appears irrational—he stares at her like he hates her and tries to change biology classes so he will not have to be her lab partner. In the typical romance pattern, their attraction is channeled through conflict, as Bella is angry at him for his unmotivated antipathy toward her. Then, also predictably, he becomes the protective hero, miraculously saving her from getting crushed by a car, an action that also reveals to Bella that he possesses supernatural qualities. None of the early stages of their romance is surprising to readers of romance, as Edward is set up predictably as stronger and more mysterious and thus more desirable than other men.

In keeping with the typical female fantasy of being desired by a man who should be unattainable, Edward tries to resist Bella, to stay away from her for her own good, but he cannot. Something about Bella—something she herself is not aware of—draws Edward too strongly. He tells her, "I got tired of trying to stay away from you."[15] And it soon becomes clear that Edward is more than a normal seventeen-year-old boy. Part of his appeal is that, in addition to being mysterious, he is potentially dangerous. In any portrayal of a plausible romantic relationship, the loved one holds a certain amount of threat to the other. This threat is usually psychological and emotional—loving makes one vulnerable to being hurt. In *Twilight*, this threat is transformed into more literal terms, as the hurt that Bella is risking by being with Edward is physical. He desires her—not just sexually, although we are told that he desires her that way as well.

The more potent desire in Edward is to drink Bella's blood. Thus, he constantly fears losing control around her: "It's not only your company I crave! Never forget *that*. Never forget I am more dangerous to you than I am to anyone else."[16] Because Edward recognizes how dangerous he can be to someone he loves, he constantly holds himself back. This is the central tension of the first novel—between his desire to feed on her and his fear of harming her. Bella is deeply desired by a man who will never let himself take her. The tension is made literal in Meyer's novels—the desire is to feed and the threat is physical—but the sexual implications are fairly obvious as the tension revolves around Edward's keeping control, not taking Bella, not penetrating her. He tells her, "You don't realize how incredibly breakable you are. I can never, never afford to lose any kind of control when I'm with you."[17]

Many online discussions have revolved around Meyer's portrayal of sexuality in the books, often concluding that the books strip Bella of any sort of sexual power and give it instead to Edward. Certainly, there is a good argument for that, as Edward is constantly withholding from Bella what she wants—sexually, emotionally, and vampirically. I would argue that, in many ways, this taps into a pervasive romantic fantasy of having a powerful, desirable man enter a woman's life and remove all responsibility, make all the difficult choices. Because Edward's hijacking of Bella's choices is all in the service of "her good," Bella can indulge in the pursuit of her desires without actually facing the consequences of achieving them. She can have it both ways.

Because Edward's vampire nature takes metaphorical form, the romantic relationship can initially be desexualized—at least in a literal sense. As I discussed earlier, Edward is compared more to an angel or a sculpture than a man, and—

although he is strong and attractive—he lacks some typical male sexual characteristics. He is cold, sparkles like crystal, and has no body hair to speak of, unlike Jacob who clearly possesses testosterone—he has all the heat, virility, and body hair that Edward doesn't.[18] One of the surprising features of the film version of *Twilight*, an adaptation that generally stayed very close to the original novel, was the appearance of Edward with a perpetual five o'clock shadow under the pale make-up. Edward's flesh in the novel is rarely described as flesh. It is like marble or diamond: pretty, shiny, and invulnerable. In *Breaking Dawn*, Bella's description of physical experience with Edward clearly describes how unfleshly it is: "I could never for a second forget that I was holding someone more angel than man in my arms."[19] Thus, through the vampire, Meyer has shaped a kind of idealized adolescent romance—being desired but not threatened by a genuine sexual relationship with a real man.

As part of this fantasy, Edward's whole existence revolves around Bella. He follows her, watches her sleep, tries to destroy himself when he thinks she is dead because "life" without her isn't worth living. Even when Edward hurts Bella, leaving her in *New Moon*, he does so only because he loves her so much.[20] Thus his breaking her heart can be considered "romantic" rather than cruel. The portrayal of Edward makes it clear that, although a certain degree of physical danger and risk in a relationship with Edward exists, Bella has nothing to fear from him. Because the fear of sex and vulnerability is made metaphorical in the figure of the vampire, the genuine risk of being in a mature, romantic relationship (being vulnerable, being hurt) is absent for Bella. Meyer has created a relationship that is ostensibly dangerous so it can possess that fantasy thrill, but it is essentially absolutely safe for Bella in all of the ways that matter.

Much of the romantic angst arises in the novel in the tension over whether or not Edward should make Bella a vampire like himself. Bella comes to the conclusion that she wants to be turned into a vampire remarkably early in their relationship. In fact, her confidence would come across as somewhat implausible, except the vampires in the Twilight Saga are clearly without any bite. Bella explains her reasoning to Edward for wanting to be a vampire by saying, "But it just seems logical . . . a man and woman have to be somewhat equal . . . as in, one of them can't always be swooping in and saving the other one. They have to save each other *equally*." Like any good romance hero, Edward replies, "You *have* saved me."[21]

In the books following *Twilight*, Bella starts to have more hesitation, although her doubts are always overshadowed by her belief in her fated love for Edward. She says in *Eclipse*, "In theory, I was anxious, even eager to trade mortality for immortality. After all, it was key to staying with Edward forever."[22] But she does start to realize that becoming a vampire would mean losing what makes her human—her own human characteristics as well as the humans she loves. However, her desire to become a vampire becomes more urgent as she ages, as she has an adolescent dread of turning nineteen while Edward is eternally seventeen. Edward is the one who resists turning Bella into a vampire, his love for her driving him to give her all the life experiences possible before he takes her life away. This tension is another way a sexual experience is explored in the novels. Like sex, becoming a vampire is a potentially dangerous experience that will completely change a woman's life. Because it is delayed by the man in this case, Bella is able to feel desirable but not have the responsibility of making the decision.

Meyer continues giving Bella the "having it both ways" fantasy as Edward is the one who wants to get married. Bella hesitates, and is thus able to feel like a modern, no-nonsense woman while still being courted in an old-fashioned way. After they get married, the issue of sex (finally in a literal sense) brings up Edward's fears again about hurting her physically. And so it is only after the marriage in *Breaking Dawn* that the tension between a man's infinite desire and infinite protection of her becomes literal. As the novels are written for a young adult audience, obviously the sex is not graphic. But the evidence of Bella's bruises and the torn pillows are visuals of this tension made manifest.[23] A more mature Bella does not want to remain in that state of tension. In fact, she enjoys sex so much she wants to delay being a vampire for it, since she is afraid her experience of sex will change once she becomes a vampire.

No Consequences

It is after the metaphorical romantic tension is resolved in literal sex that the nature of the narrative takes a sharp turn. Instead of a "safe" metaphor, the story becomes remarkably more graphic with Bella's pregnancy and the resulting birth. The scenes of Bella with the half-vampire baby inside of her, killing her, feeding on her, causing her to drink blood, are all told through Jacob's eyes. Because Jacob's perspective is negative about the whole experience, he emphasizes the unnatural, disgusting aspects of it. Bella writhes and vomits fountains of blood, graphic images like nothing we saw in the previous books. Many readers resented the shift in the final book, and that is hardly surprising. But it does seem to be in keeping with the pattern of the metaphorical becoming literal.

Bella tells Jacob that she has "faith" that "this is all going somewhere good."[24] And she isn't wrong. Because, despite the more graphic nature of *Breaking Dawn*, the narrative continues the pattern set up in the first three books of fulfilling fantasies by having it both ways. All of the potential dangers and sacrifices that come with becoming a vampire are removed, so Bella is able to indulge in even this experience in a way that becomes perfectly safe for her.

She is turned into a vampire after giving birth to Renesmee, and her initial experiences are positive ones. Once Bella becomes a vampire, all of her senses heighten and she is able to better experience and appreciate the world. Before she was turned, she feared being at the mercy of her carnal, violent instincts for human blood, but instead she maintains her free will even as a newborn vampire. Edward is amazed by her self-control. He says,

> You shouldn't be able to do any of this. You shouldn't be so rational. You shouldn't be able to stand here discussing this with me calmly and coolly. And, much more than any of that, you should not have been able to break off mid-hunt with the scent of human blood in the air. Even mature vampires have difficulty with that—we're always careful of where we hunt so as not to put ourselves in the path of temptation. Bella, you're behaving like you're decades rather than days old.[25]

Not only is she able to keep from doing what she understands as morally wrong, but she is also able to be a vampire and still keep her human loved ones in her life, including Charlie, her father, whom she always assumed she would lose when she was turned. The book recognizes how unusual this is—Bella claims she must have a superpower by being able to keep Charlie in her life—but this ability takes away all negative consequences of her turning vampire. In fact, Bella says, "I was amazing now—to them and to myself. It was like I had been born to be a vampire. The idea made me want to laugh, but it also made me want to sing. I had found my true place

in the world, the place I fit, the place I shined."[26] In pure
fantasy style, Bella is able to have everything, eternal life with
Edward and none of the negative implications it should have
brought with it.[27]

Destined Love and Family

Instead of using the vampire to explore theological or metaphysical themes, the major themes in the Twilight Saga are
explicitly human: family and destined, romantic love. Meyer
uses the vampire to embody these themes, themes we could
also see in earlier vampire stories. But, unlike those earlier
examples, she does not explore them in any sort of spiritual
way. The result is entirely secular. Thus the portrayal of the
vampire is, not coincidentally, a very domesticated, defanged
version.

The novels take Bella through the process of finding and
forming her own family. She is isolated at the beginning. She
has a mother and a father, but they are divorced and she seems
alienated from a real family unit. The vampires she meets
have formed their own family: Carlisle and Esme and their
"adopted" children have become the Cullen family, a family
designed by their own free will. Bella soon thinks of them
as her family and she also finds a different sort of family in
Jacob's pack. In *Breaking Dawn*, the story is about bringing
her whole family together: vampires, natural family (Charlie),
werewolves, and then a literal family with Edward and their
daughter, Renesmee. Near the end of the book, the vampire
Garrett vocalizes how significant these family connections
are in the vampire experience:

> These strange golden-eyed ones deny their very natures. But in
> return they have found something worth even more, perhaps,

than mere gratification of desire. I've made a little study of them in my time here, and it seems to me that intrinsic to this intense family binding—that which makes them possible at all—is the peaceful character of this life of sacrifice.[28]

While the theme of family is handled in a rather simplistic way, it is certainly a dominant theme in the books.[29]

The more dominant theme is, of course, romantic love. More than anything else, the Twilight books are romance novels—of the adolescent variety. As I discussed early, the working out of Bella's romantic relationship fulfills a certain kind of female fantasy. But it also contributes to the overall themes of the novels. Not long after she meets him, Bella is able to say, "About three things I was absolutely positive. First, Edward was a vampire. Second, there was a part of him—and I didn't know how potent that part might be—that thirsted for my blood. And third, I was unconditionally and irrevocably in love with him."[30] And this love she feels, while we can certainly doubt whether the portrayal is realistic in terms of human social and psychological plausibility, is understood as true and absolute in the world of the novel.[31]

The love Bella feels for Edward becomes the most important feature of her life. She says at the end of *Twilight*, "Besides, since I'd come to Forks, it really seemed like my life was *about* him."[32] It is more important than her friends, her family, her health, her self-esteem, her future. When she goes into significant depression after Edward leaves her in *New Moon*, Charlie tries to encourage her to spend time with friends, to better balance her life, and she only partially agrees with this assessment. Romantic love, as it is represented in the books, is more important than anything else. In *New Moon*, she even tells Edward that she prioritizes her love above any sort of spiritual reality: "This is about my soul, isn't it? . . .

I don't care! You can have my soul. I don't want it without you—it's yours already!"[33]

Her love also transcends any moral compass she might have. While she is briefly bothered from time to time that Edward might have killed people in his past as a vampire, this concern is minimal and quickly overcome. She says, as a way of explaining it away, "Love is irrational, I reminded myself. The more you loved someone, the less sense anything made."[34] In *Eclipse*, when Edward and Bella discuss *Wuthering Heights* and Edward complains that none of the characters have any redeeming qualities, Bella says, quite astutely, "Their love *is* their only redeeming quality."[35] While certainly true of *Wuthering Heights*, this statement can also be true of the Twilight Saga. Romantic love, as the books represent it, is so absolute and transcendent that it overwhelms any other moral or social questions.

Ironically, in a series that emphasizes human free will over any spiritual or theological issue, romantic love is the one aspect of life where the characters lose their free will. Edward tries to pull away from Bella more than once, but his love always draws him back—even though his free will tells him spending time with her is wrong. Bella never doubts that as soon as Edward entered her life, her whole world changed irrevocably. And in the werewolf community, we see another picture of how romantic love means losing the ability to choose. Werewolves will sometimes imprint on a female—some sort of instinctive marking of the woman as theirs. Imprinting is irreversible and outside of the individual's control. In fact, Bella's werewolf friend Jacob says in *Breaking Dawn* that imprinting is "just another way of getting your choices taken away from you."[36] He hates the concept when he makes that claim, but later he himself imprints—on Edward and Bella's baby, Renesmee. He falls in love with Renesmee through some undefined cosmic design rather than through his own choice. While the relationship is clearly desexualized until the girl has matured, his free will about love is indeed taken away. He had always chosen to love Bella, but his choice in the future about whom he will love is made for him. The reason this is palatable, to Jacob and to readers, is that he seems to enjoy the lack of free will in this aspect of his life. And certainly it works out better for everyone, since Bella has never been able to choose him. But love, throughout, is the one thing in the novels that seems to be predestined and outside of human free will.

Since these are romance novels, it is not necessarily surprising. But it does end up completely secularizing the figure of the vampire, who traditionally has been used to explore spiritual free will and moral choice. Instead of using the vampire to explore the nature of the soul, an individual's eternal condition, and the place of evil in the world and in individual lives, it is used in the Twilight Saga to explore romance and the nature of romantic love.

In Peter and Eli Fosl's essay, "*Vampire-Dämmerung*: What Can *Twilight* Tell Us about God?" the authors conclude that Bella and Edward find happiness, not through the natural order of creation dictated by a traditional concept of God, but through relying on their own "unnatural" choices—they are able to achieve happiness on their own.[37] This is an astute reading of the novels, emphasizing both the emphasis on pure free will in the Twilight Saga and the irrelevance of a theological framework for Meyer's narrative. As the vampire has become an idealized romantic superhero, he has lost his potential for spiritual and theological reflection. He has also become rather tame, repressed, pretty, glittery, and vegetarian. He has lost his fangs.

123

7

Vampire Sinners

> When you understand the nature of a thing, you know what it's capable of.
>
> Blade in the film *Blade*

Robert Rodriquez's 1996 film *From Dusk Till Dawn*, with a screenplay written by Quentin Tarantino, initially looks nothing like a vampire film. The first half of the movie focuses only on human violence and crime. Brothers Seth (George Clooney) and Richie (Tarantino) are blazing their way through a crime spree: robbing banks, murdering both police and civilians, and kidnapping without hesitation or conscience. Seth prides himself on being a professional, while Richie just mindlessly thrives on blood and violence. On their way to Mexico, the brothers kidnap a preacher named Jacob who has lost his faith in God (Harvey Keitel) and his two teenage children (Ernest Liu and Juliette Lewis) in order to use the family's RV to get across the border. Only when they reach a sleazy Mexican bar—a rendezvous point where Seth will meet a friend—does the film morph from a crime thriller (not a thoughtful one) into a vampire horror film. The bar is full of vampires. In this horrific setting, man's inhumanity to man no longer matters, as the characters are faced with something truly inhuman. Strangers, criminals, and former victims must suddenly become allies. Lost faith must be found again because the world has suddenly transformed from what it appeared to be only minutes before.

While the film is mostly a string of excessive violence—walking a line between tongue-in-cheek cynicism and exploitative entertainment—*From Dusk Till Dawn* is worth considering in an examination of vampires in contemporary culture. Despite its irony and overblown gruesomeness, the film constructs a mostly traditional portrait of the vampire. The vampires in the film are monstrous, demonic, and inhuman. Once bitten, a person is as good as dead, even if it takes a while for the transformation into monster to take place.

Holy objects are effective in fighting them, although these are also used with thick irony. Jacob makes a cross out of a gun and blesses water to be used in a water gun and water balloons against the vampires. With these unlikely weapons, the desperate humans have to fight the unholy vampires, sending them "back to hell."[1] In a rather perverse affirmation of religious belief, even Seth—the conscienceless criminal—must conjure up a faith in God in order to fight the vampires. As in traditional vampire stories, the vampire in this movie is also connected to temptation. Salma Hayek plays an exotic dancer, Satanico Pandemonium, who slinks her way through an erotic dance with an albino snake before she reveals herself to be a vampire.

The film, however—like many contemporary vampire tales—is not really interested in exploring human sin. The vampire represents evil, but it is an evil clearly distinct from humanity. Richie is killed in the fight with the vampires, but Seth survives with the stolen money. Kate, the teenage daughter, is the only one of her family to survive, and she actually wants to stay with her abductor—evidently overlooking the fact that Seth kidnapped her. He is not a vampire, and that puts him on her side. While the characters summon up "faith" to fight the vampires, it has absolutely no effect on behavior or human experience once the vampires are defeated. All humans are shown to be sympathetic, at least when compared to vampires. So, what had the potential to be an exploration of sin by using the figure of the vampire is actually the opposite—a horror movie that suggests human evil is nothing compared to what a real monster might do to you.

We have seen in previous chapters how the vampire has become less and less of a representation of sin as the figure becomes increasingly secularized. In this chapter, I will examine a few more examples of vampire stories, focusing specifically on how the stories use the vampire in regard to the issue of sin. The early Dracula films still take the concept of sin seriously, reflecting Stoker's original novel. The theme just becomes minimized through the way the narrative portrays the central vampire acts and through a focus on mood and suspense rather than theme. Another way to see the idea of sin explored in vampire stories is by looking at the idea of a half-vampire hybrid. In narratives that work with this concept, the human blood of the hybrid has the potential to overcome the evil vampire influence—which allows a compromise between a more traditional portrayal of sin and an emphasis on human free will. And, finally, by looking at examples of vampire stories that deal with vampires in a community, we can see how the idea of sin can be transformed completely into amorality, as vampires become a law unto themselves. Because sin was one of the fundamental concepts associated with vampires in early stories, it has not completely disappeared. We can still see sin represented and transformed through a wide variety of vampire stories.

Early Dracula Films

In 1931, Bela Lugosi played Dracula in a tradition-shaping performance—one that has been nearly as influential on popular conception of the vampire as Stoker's novel itself. The film *Dracula*, directed by Tod Browning, stays close to the original novel in many ways. Instead of Jonathon Harker as the original visitor to Castle Dracula, the film places Renfield (Dwight Frye) in that role. Many of the details of Lucy's descent into the "Bloofer Lady" are left out. And the film does not end with a frantic race across Europe and Asia. The basics of the plot and theme of the film, however, are in keeping with Stoker's. It also sustains many of the religious elements. One of the first shots shows a cross on a hill as Renfield approaches the inn in Transylvania.

Following that introduction, the symbol of the crucifix is used throughout the film—a more potent deterrent to the vampire than other weapons, such as the poisonous herb wolfsbane. Unlike the ugly, unnatural Dracula of the novel, Bela Lugosi plays the Count as sophisticated and darkly fascinating, with a voice that is both seductive and creepy. The vampire assaults are subtly eroticized in the film—through a number of images that juxtapose a small, pale, female form with the dark, looming vampire, who leans over her in almost an embrace. The film even incorporates one of the most important lines from the novel. Early at Castle Dracula, the Count says, "The blood is the life, Mr. Renfield."[2] So most of the symbolic elements we saw in the novel *Dracula* are present in the film.

But the symbolism and spiritual significance of these elements are minimized by the way the film constantly cuts away at the crucial moments. We do not actually see Dracula assaulting the woman in the street. We see him lean forward, but then the scene ends abruptly. We also do not see Dracula assault Lucy (Francis Dade). The scene shows him as a bat outside her window, then suddenly crouching over her bed. He reaches out to her neck. Then the shot ends. While there is certainly a kind of power in leaving graphic acts unseen, the constant cutaways make the vampire more about mood, suspense, and fear than about the actual act of drinking blood. It is in the act itself that much of the theological significance lies, and the blood itself becomes almost irrelevant in the film. What is more important is the vague, mostly unseen threat posed by the vampire.

The film is also stripped of any real climax. Van Helsing (Edward Van Sloan) and Harker's (David Manners) trip over to the abbey to kill Dracula has no traditional buildup through rising action. Because Dracula is sleeping, there is no genuine threat to them at that point. We do not even see Van Helsing drive the stake into Dracula's heart. In the novel, the narrative built up to the climax through an increasingly heightened Christian mission against evil. The film does not do so. While the film is beautiful, powerful, and influential in many ways and sustains—at least on the surface—many of the novel's themes, it does not explore the theological issues with any depth, which is an early step toward the process of secularization.

Universal Studios released three other Dracula films in the thirties and forties. The first of these was Lambert Hillyer's *Dracula's Daughter* (1936). The film begins with Van Helsing (again played by Edward Van Sloan) being arrested for staking Dracula. Countess Marya Zaleska (Gloria Holden) soon makes an appearance, and she calls herself Dracula's daughter. This is an early portrait of the vampire with a conscience, or at least some guilt over her evil actions. The Countess wants to be "free to live as a woman"[3] and no longer be cursed with her vampire nature. She burns Dracula's body in a sort of ritual, casting out the evil spirit while holding the symbol of the cross. When she seeks the aid of the psychiatrist Dr. Garth (Otto Kruger), he articulates the tension she embodies as the "strength of the human mind against the powers of darkness."[4] Despite the Countess's desire to be free, the film sustains the nature of the vampire as a damned one—she cannot free herself of her nature and ends up kidnapping the woman Garth loves in order to tempt Garth into Transylvania, where she wants him to become a vampire like herself. The film adds a layer of complexity to the vampire nature by allowing the Countess to feel guilt and desire, but it still portrays the vampire as a symbol for sin, which will forever pull the individual back into evil.

The 1943 film *Son of Dracula* conveys less complexity in the portrayal of the vampire than *Dracula's Daughter*. Count Alucard (*Dracula* spelled backward, played by Lon Chaney Jr.) is a seductive and mesmerizing figure and is invited on a trip to America. There he tempts and marries a southern girl, Katherine, in order to gain her estate. The twist of the plot is that Katherine is actually trying to use Alucard in order to gain the vampire's immortality. The cross is again significant in the film, although a gesture is made at a rational explanation for its effectiveness. Professor Lazio (J. Edward Bromberg) says, "It would take too long to explain why they fear it [the cross], but they do."[5] The resolution of the film affirms the nature of the vampire established in the earlier films. The vampire nature is an evil one, and it cannot be used to serve human purposes without serious consequences.

In the 1945 film *House of Dracula*, we again have a vampire who ostensibly wants to defy his nature. Count Dracula (John Carradine) comes to a scientist and asks to be released from his "misery," from the curse of being a vampire.[6] The scientist has an experimental procedure with spores and blood transfusions (a procedure that successfully cures the Wolf Man) and attempts to make an antitoxin for the vampire's blood. But just as in the earlier films, the nature of the vampire is not able to be overcome. Whether or not Dracula was sincere in his wish to change, he is unable to do so. He seduces the scientist's assistant and—though briefly halted by the cross—convinces her to throw the crucifix off the balcony when she makes a choice to be with him. He is ultimately unsuccessful and is destroyed, but not before the scientist's blood is contaminated by Dracula's and the man becomes a monster himself. The scientist articulates his condition by saying his soul has been taken over by lust, by an evil thing—a thing that must be destroyed.

In all of these films, the original Christian vampire themes of temptation and the fight against evil are sustained—they are just not as strongly developed. The films instead prioritize atmosphere, mood, and suspense. They portray the vampire nature as a monstrous one—it cannot be overcome, even if the vampire itself wishes it to be. As in Stoker's novel, the cross is always the surest protection against the vampire. And the films also develop another theme we see in Stoker, one that explores modern scientific thinking in relation to superstition. Although humans might try to understand the supernatural through the lens of a scientific worldview, science is never enough to fully understand and address the supernatural power. In *House of Dracula*, science might have cured the Wolf Man, but it also ended up contaminating the scientist with vampire blood and turning him into a monster.

Science might help, but it simply is not enough in the fight
against sin and evil.

Half-Vampire Hybrids

One way to navigate the tension between traditional characterization and the desire for enough complexity in the vampire
to explore issues of free will is to pose the possibility of half-
vampires or hybrid creatures—somewhere between vampire
and human. These half-vampires are most commonly referred
to now as *dhampirs*, a word from Balkan folklore. Two examples of the way these half-vampires can be handled are
Blade, a film series loosely based on a series of Marvel comics,
and *Vampire Hunter D*, a cult-favorite anime film based on
a series of Japanese illustrated novels written by Hideyuki
Kikuchi and illustrated by Yoshitaka Amano. Both examples
maintain pure vampires as monstrous. The half-vampires
have the best of both worlds in terms of characteristics—all
of the abilities of vampires without many of the vampire
weaknesses. And, through the idea of mixed blood, the creators of these half-vampires are able to explore issues of sin
through the vampire while still focusing on human free will.

Because the half-vampire characters allow for a more complex portrait of guilt and temptation, the full vampires in
these representations are often completely monstrous. One
of the early scenes of the film *Blade* (1998) shows a human
man following a beautiful woman into what he thinks is a
wild party or a rave. The man soon learns differently, however, when blood starts to spray from the ceiling and he is
suddenly surrounded by vampires, ready to drink his blood.
When the half-vampire hero Blade (Wesley Snipes) arrives to
fight the vampires, everyone is covered and dripping with the
spraying blood, a graphic image of the vampire's monstrous

nature. The plot of the film centers on the plans of a radical vampire named Frost, who is frustrated with vampire politics and the hierarchy of the pure-born vampires who look down on him because he was turned rather than born a vampire. Frost discovers a way to awaken La Magra, a vampire god who will aid him in his quest for vampire dominance in the world. While the vampires in the film certainly have some human qualities—pride, ambition, conflict, and the like—they are only interested in feeding their desires and in destruction. They are not sanitized or domesticated, and their purpose is to represent an evil that must be fought.

The 1985 anime film *Vampire Hunter D* portrays true vampires similarly. Both the novels and the film are set in a far-future earth—around AD 12,090—where nuclear war nearly destroyed human society and let vampires and other monsters take over. The chief villain of the film is Magnus Lee, a ten-thousand-year-old vampire who is a descendant of Count Dracula. Magnus Lee is sophisticated but purely evil, controlling hosts of vicious monsters—including werewolves and three snake women—and ruthlessly trying to make a mortal girl his bride. There is no real possibility of mercy or kindness for the true vampires in these stories. They are traditional portraits of vampires as demons, rather than the softer, gentler vampires of many other contemporary books and movies.

The complexity in vampire characterization in these stories results from the portrayal of the half-vampire hybrids. In *Blade*, the title character's mother was bitten by a vampire while she was pregnant with him. Thus he becomes a kind of vampire hybrid. In the original Marvel comics, he has the vampire characteristics of an extended lifespan and a sensitivity to the supernatural—plus an immunity to becoming a full vampire. In the film, the character also has a vampire's

133

strength and skills, as well as a thirst for their blood. He does not, however, have any of the typical weaknesses. He can go out in the daytime and is not allergic to garlic, for instance. Vampire Hunter D is in a similar situation. He is the son of a human woman and a vampire man (later revealed to be Dracula himself). He has the vampire grace, speed, and strength but only mild levels of their weaknesses—and, as such, he does not fit in anywhere, forced to walk between worlds. He also has a sentient left hand, who talks to him, mocks him, and gives advice. Both Blade and D try to overcome their vampire blood by actively taking on the role of vampire hunter, killing vampires and saving humans from vampire violence.

Despite their attempts to do good, both characters are torn by their dual natures and still struggle with their blood thirst. Blade, in the film, must continually be injected with higher and higher doses of a serum that suppresses his thirst for blood. But the film makes it clear that eventually this serum will no longer work. In the film *Vampire Hunter D*, D is attracted to the human girl Doris, but when he gets close to her his fangs come out and he has to resist the desire to bite her. Both characters, however, find victory over their partial vampire natures through an exertion of free will. Similar to the full vampires in Harris and Meyer, these hybrid vampires are able to choose to do good and be human rather than succumb to their vampire blood and do evil. It is a struggle for both of them, but it is possible.

So, one way to maintain the traditional vampire characterization—that of an evil demon or monster—and still allow for the theme of sin and free will is to portray these half-vampire hybrids. Like the character of Angel in *Buffy*, the human side is strong enough to fight against the vampire side. This allows for a metaphorical exploration of the human fight against sin and evil.

Vampires in Community: Laws unto Themselves

In Charlaine Harris's *Dead Until Dark*, the vampire Bill tells Sookie that vampires who live in "nests"—in community—become crueler and less human than vampires who live alone. Bill explains, "They see others like themselves constantly, and so they are reminded how far from human they are. They become laws unto themselves."[7] Although this statement is made within the mythology of Harris's Southern Vampire Mysteries, it also very aptly expresses the portrayal of vampires in community that is often found in other stories in popular culture. In the last couple of decades, the figure of the vampire has often been used to explore the concept of community, dealing with questions of identity, conflict, and history. In the 2003 film *Underworld* and its sequels and the 1996 television show *Kindred: The Embraced* (based on the role-playing game *Vampire: The Masquerade*), we can see representative examples of how vampires are often depicted in community. In both of these tales, the vampire community is given an elaborate history and mythology, there is a noticeable lack of religious elements, and the vampire society creates its own system of morality—distinct from human and particularly Christian morality. These two examples provide good illustrations of how, when vampires are placed in community in popular culture, the concept of sin itself becomes obsolete as the vampires become laws unto themselves.

Whenever vampires are used in a narrative, it is necessary to establish the distinct mythology and the rules governing the vampire's existence and characteristics. When the portrait of vampires focuses on community rather than vampires as individuals, often the history and mythology become more elaborate and more deeply emphasized in the story. *Kindred: The Embraced*, a television show that aired on Fox for less than a season in the mid-'90s, produced by John Leekley and

Aaron Spelling, had a distinct mythology for its vampires built around a number of vampire "clans." Because the show was based on a role-playing game, the clan characteristics were well-developed and the relationships between them preestablished. Vampires in this fictional world, who call themselves Kindred, exist in clans, determined by the clan of the vampire that turned them.

These clans each have distinct characteristics. The Ventrue are patrician and sophisticated, and often the Prince comes from this clan—like Julian (Mark Frankel), the handsome, elegant Prince of San Francisco and lead character of the series. The Gangrels are gypsy-like, rebellious, and often seen riding motorcycles. The Brujah are tough and thuggish, while the Toreadors tend to be artists and entertainers. The Nosferatu clan takes the vampire's primitive form (inspired by the film of the same name) and thus cannot be mistaken for human, so they live mostly underground. Each clan within a city has a leader called a Primogen, and each city has a Prince, who leads the clans and attempts to keep peace. The vampires are able to survive by hiding their existence among humans, an elaborate ruse they call the "Masquerade." The show explores how the vampires exist in these clans, how the clans relate to each other, and how they manage to exist within human society. Thus, the complex mythology is the central focus of the narrative.

The film *Underworld* and its two sequels, *Underworld: Evolution* and *Underworld: The Rise of the Lycans*, are similar in the way the films' mythology and history are more important than the individual characters. *Underworld* is also set in a world where vampires live in their own communities within the larger human society. The chief purpose of these vampires is not to drink human blood—in fact, they seem to live on synthetic or cloned blood and seldom attack humans.

The only blood-drinking scene in the first film is between the vampire Kraven (Shane Brolley) and Erica (Sophia Myles), another vampire, during sex. The vampires are in a centuries-old war with Lycans, werewolves—who actually share their bloodline. The history of the films establishes Alexander Corvinus as the shared ancestor of both breeds. Corvinus managed to survive a plague, which mutated his blood to make him immortal. Two of his sons were also immortal, and one was bitten by a bat (creating vampires) and one by a wolf (creating Lycans). His human son remained mortal but passed on a strain of the virus to his descendants, including Michael Corvin (Scott Speedman), one of the main characters in the film.

The plot of the first film centers around the Lycan attempt to create a hybrid of vampire and Lycan, only possible through Michael Corvin, who has the original Corvinus virus in his blood. This backstory not only dominates the plots of the films, but it also takes much of the supernatural out of the figure of the vampire. Since vampires (and Lycans) are the result of a virus, then science is able to explain their existence—in a way that the early Dracula films played with but ultimately resisted.

In both *Kindred: The Embraced* and the *Underworld* films, religion is virtually absent. While in both stories, the vampires are nourished and sustained by blood, the blood drinking is not given the normal symbolic significance. In the first episode of *Kindred: The Embraced*, there is a scene where the vampire Alexandra (Kate Vernon) goes into the ladies room and drinks the blood of a human victim. The act does not kill the woman, and Alexandra hypnotizes her into forgetting what happened. The camera focuses on a drop of blood on Alexandra's white top afterward, but that is one of the only incidents of the kind in the short run of the show.

For the most part, the focus of *Kindred* is on social issues of clan conflict, ambition, and secrecy. In the final episode, "Cabin in the Woods," the Ventrue vampire Archon (Patrick Bachau), former Prince and Julian's mentor and maker, is killed by the Brujah vampire Cameron (Titus Welliver) in revenge for Archon's slaughter of innocent Brujah decades earlier. Archon willingly surrenders to Cameron, stretching out both arms in an obvious allusion to the crucifixion. But, despite the Christ reference, Archon is not a Christ figure. He explicitly says his death will pay the debt he owes for his own guilt—he is not dying for someone else's guilt—and the emphasis is still on social issues of justice and vengeance, rather than on anything theological. The show has almost entirely taken the figure of the vampire out of any religious or theological context.

In the *Underworld* films, we see the same dynamic. Blood drinking is not the central vampire act in the films. The vampire warriors, or Death Dealers, as they're called, kill primarily with guns and other weapons. As I mentioned earlier, in the first film there is only one image of a vampire drinking blood from someone else—and that is the blood of another vampire and is a sexual act rather than an assault. Within the mythology of the show, drinking the blood of another vampire allows that vampire to "remember" the history of the other vampire, so it is a means of sharing knowledge. Feeding on blood is never portrayed as violence, temptation, or guilt in the films. In fact, in *Underworld: Evolution*, Selene (Kate Beckinsale) tells Michael that if he doesn't feed on the manufactured blood, his hunger will get the best of him and he'll feed on a human—and Michael doesn't "want that on his conscience."[8] There is no religious content in the films at all. In *Underworld: Evolution*, Selene and Michael visit Tanis (Steven Mackintosh), who has been exiled in an old monastery. But Tanis has used his time in exile to enjoy himself, and he is shown as having an orgy in the building, turning the religious setting into something carnal. As in *Kindred: The Embraced*, the vampires are used to explore social issues rather than religious ones.

In both stories, this focus on the social rather than religious or theological leads to the vampire communities constructing their own moral systems. Since they function in a community of their own kind, rather than the larger human community, they create their own standards of right and wrong behavior. In *Kindred: The Embraced*, the vampires are supposed to obey human law. This is not because any of the vampires believe that human law has real power over them, but because it is the only way to maintain the Masquerade, to keep their existence secret. When Frank (C. Thomas Howell), a police detective on a mission to bring down the Kindred community, confronts Julian about breaking the law, Julian replies, "Your morality doesn't apply to us. I am the law among my kind. The judge, the jury, and the executioner."[9] The vampires decide for themselves what constitutes crime and what needs to be punished. So the death of Alexandra is justified by their moral system, because she threatened the Masquerade by revealing the vampire's existence to Frank. And when Cameron kills Archon, no one can object to the deed, not even Julian the Prince, because it was an act of lawful vengeance and thus justified by their moral standards. Because vampires exist in community, they create their own systems of morality—so we don't see the overriding guilt that is commonly a part of the figure of the vampire.

In *Underworld* too the human concept of law or morality is irrelevant. In fact, human society as a whole takes a backseat to the society of vampires and Lycans. Because the vampires are involved in a longstanding war against Lycans, anything that aids their cause seems to be justified. So to open gunfire in a crowded subway terminal is acceptable, even if it puts the humans surrounding them at risk. Because vampires have free will, they can choose to not kill humans, which Selene at least chooses. But within the justification of their war, all else seems to be allowable. In fact, the biggest threat that the vampire poses is not the supernatural threats of blood drinking or hypnosis, but rather the very human threats of betrayal and deception. Selene and Michael spend most of their time in the films protecting themselves and fighting against Kraven, the vampire traitor, and Marcus (Tony Curran), the vampire elder who sought to free his brother (the first Lycan) and thus wreak havoc on the world.

In both *Kindred: The Embraced* and *Underworld*, vampires are more often a danger to other vampires than they are to humans. They exist in their own communities, and so all the traditional themes connected to their interaction with humans are minimized or removed. They are not sinners in the traditional sense because they do not follow human morality. They become a law unto themselves.

Because sin has traditionally been associated with the figure of the vampire, it remains in various forms, even in stories that have other purposes. Sometimes it is minimized in favor of building fear and suspense, as we see in the early Dracula films from Universal Studios. Sometimes it is represented through the conflict between the human side and the vampire side of half-vampire hybrid characters. The concept of sin can also be transformed into an entirely different system of vampire morality, where what humans might consider sin becomes acceptable within the vampire community. Vampires have long been representations of sin. As we will see in the next chapter, a rising trend in popular culture is to cast the vampire in the role not of sinner but of one who saves.

140

8

Vampire Saviors

We all got something to atone for.

Doyle in "City of"
(*Angel*, season 1)

A few years after Anne Rice published *Interview with the Vampire*, Chelsea Quinn Yarbro began another very popular vampire series—the Saint-Germain vampire series. The first novel, *Hôtel Transylvania* (1978), introduced the series hero, le Comte de Saint-Germain. Saint-Germain in the novels is a vampire but is based on a genuine historical man: a courtier, adventurer, musician, and alchemist in the eighteenth century with a mysterious life and identity. Yarbro explains that she wanted to shape the figure of the vampire in a way that kept some of the traditional characteristics based in folklore and mythology—the drinking of blood and need for native earth, for example—but lost the Christian associations that vampire lore had developed. So Saint-Germain is not evil or demonic. He is, in fact, a sympathetic hero.

The novels play up the historic Saint-Germain's associations with the occult, but the narrative makes it clear that this occult power is not necessarily associated with Satan or evil. In *Hôtel Transylvania*, Saint-Germain explains to Madelaine, the young heroine of the novel:

> There is a Power, which is only that. It is like the rivers, which nurture us and can destroy us. Whether we are prosperous or drowned in flood-waters, the rivers are still the same. So with this Power. And when it lifts us up and opens our eyes to goodness and wonders, so that we are ennobled and inspired to kindness and excellence, we call it God. But when it is used for pain and suffering and degradation, we call it Satan. The Power is both. It is our use alone which makes it one or the other.[1]

When Madelaine calls his words heresy by the standards of the church, Saint-Germain merely replies, "It is the truth."[2] Once she realizes that Saint-Germain is a vampire and succumbs to her desire to let him feed on her, Madelaine later justifies the act by comparing the vampiric experience to a sacrament of the church, because both revolve around the drinking of blood.

Like Edward in *Twilight*, Saint-Germain knows that he poses a certain danger to Madelaine because of his desire for her, but he is able to drink blood in a way that does not threaten her life. In fact, it brings her pleasure and is clearly turned into a sexual experience, although it is not connected with actual intercourse, the way it is in novels like Charlaine Harris's. Throughout the novel, Saint-Germain consistently distinguishes himself from those who worship Satan and use occult power for pain and suffering. The plot of *Hôtel Tran-*

sylvania centers on the conflict between him and true worshipers of the devil. Although he is a vampire, he is good, and he is not in any way associated with genuine evil or darkness.

Yarbro, like Rice, is one of the early artists who makes the vampire into a sympathetic figure. While one trend in contemporary vampire portrayals deals with vampires as sinners in one way or the other, another trend shapes them into heroes, or saviors. In this chapter, I will examine a few ways this happens in a sampling of vampire stories. One way is to portray a vampire who is seeking redemption by doing good and being a hero. Other vampire stories place the vampire in a romance and make the vampire a suitable romantic partner. And, in the novels of Laurel K. Hamilton, we can see another possibility, where the vampire represents a kind of amoral power which, like in Yarbro, can be channeled for both good and evil. What all of these stories have in common is the way they turn the vampire from sinner and villain into, instead, someone with the potential to be a hero.

Lone Vampires on a Quest for Redemption

One way we see the figure of the vampire in popular culture is as a lonely figure striving endlessly for redemption by actively doing good in the world. Two representative examples of this are in one of the earliest vampire television shows, *Forever Knight*, and later in the *Buffy* spin-off series *Angel*. Both shows are built around a repentant vampire who wants to atone for his misdeeds, and both vampires become crime fighters as a result of this pursuit of redemption. In both shows, the vampire has a history of sin to overcome, religion is at issue but is not the central focus, and the vampire uses his particular gifts and characteristics in order to do good instead of evil.

The lead vampires in both series have a history of sin to overcome. From the first episode of *Forever Knight*, we become acquainted with the history of sin that the vampire Knight has to deal with. The first scene of the series begins in a candlelit castle in Paris in 1228, setting up Nick Knight's (Geraint Wyn Davies) initiation into vampirehood with his mentor LaCroix (Nigel Bennett) and fellow vampire Janette (Deborah Duchêne). The other two vampires offer Knight a beautiful young woman. Throughout that first episode, Knight keeps returning to that memory—reminding himself of his true nature as a vampire and the evil it demanded of him in the past. Throughout the series, Knight's memories keep reemerging and become both a torment and a goad to do good, to make amends for his past. The premise of the show is that Knight is trying to become mortal again—his friend/romantic interest, Dr. Natalie Lambert (Catherine Disher), tries to help him achieve mortality by encouraging him to give up drinking blood. But his desire for blood is set up as an addiction, and he constantly struggles to fight against his vampire urge.

Angel (David Boreanaz) too on the television series *Angel* is struggling to overcome his vampire nature and atone for his sins from the past. Because his character originated on *Buffy the Vampire Slayer*, his history is more complicated and well-developed than Knight's. On *Forever Knight*, the vampire possesses a free will to a certain extent—he has chosen to try to do good instead of evil. For Angel, his work toward atonement is only possible because he possesses a human soul to counteract the vampire demon inside him.

The show works with the history of Angel established on *Buffy*, and so viewers know from the beginning the sins Angel has to deal with. And throughout the show, just as on *Forever Knight*, Angel flashes back to pieces of his history and is confronted with the evil he committed as Angelus. In the first episode of the series, Doyle (Glenn Quinn) approaches Angel and tells him that the "Powers That Be," nameless figures who are somehow involved in the destiny of the world, have summoned Doyle to help Angel. Angel has wallowed in his nature for so long that he is "cut off" from those he is trying to help, Doyle says.[3] Instead, Angel needs to learn to reach out to those people, feel for them and empathize with them. Through that, Doyle explains, Angel can find hope again. That is the premise of the show, very much like that of *Forever Knight*: a repentant vampire seeking to actively help other people. Knight does it through his job as a police detective and Angel through the establishment of a kind of detective agency where he can do supernatural-type jobs to aid those who need his help. When Angel asks Doyle why he is helping him, Doyle explains the thematic premise of the show: "We all got something to atone for."[4]

Because of the theme of atonement and redemption, religion is at issue in both shows, although it is not the central issue connected to the figure of the vampire. *Forever Knight* is much more explicitly Christian than *Angel*. For instance, in the first-season episode "For I Have Sinned," Knight has to investigate a crime connected to a church. The set-up of the plot shows a woman having sex in a furniture store and then leaving and putting on a cross necklace and her engagement ring—establishing sin as a spiritual reality. The woman immediately gets murdered, the killer telling her as she dies that she "doesn't deserve to wear" the cross. The killer calls himself the "arm of God" and God's "fury."[5] As Knight is called in to investigate this series of killings, he has to overcome his vampire aversion to the church, the cross, and other holy objects, and he has to reconcile the unnatural immortality he has found as a vampire with the spiritual immortality to be found in God.

The flashbacks in this episode take him back in memory to a conversation he had with Joan of Arc, who refuses his offer to make her a vampire, asks him about his faith, and encourages him that his lost faith is always there to regain. The episode uses the Christian foundation of the vampire myth and takes it seriously. As a picture of a sinner, Knight is burned by the cross, explaining that it is a "symbol of the one true light" while vampires are "creatures of the dark."[6] While the series as a whole uses the figure of the vampire to explore ideas of addiction and dependence more than Christian faith, it is certainly a more traditional take than those that come after it, including the series *Angel*.

In *Angel*, too, religion is at issue, although the religion in the show is much less traditionally Christian than on *Forever Knight*. *Angel* rarely explores the concepts surrounding the Christian cross or holy objects with any depth, although Angel cannot come into contact with a cross and is not particularly fond of churches. In the first-season episode "Somnambulist," we learn that when Angel was Angelus—a vampire without a soul—he would carve a cross into the chests of his victims as a way of mocking God. When a vampire he "mentored" in the past arrives in Los Angeles and starts marking his kills in the same way, Angel must confront his own evil nature, despite the ways the soul has changed him and given him the potential to do good. The episode includes the memorable image of Angel squeezing a cross until his skin burns. In his conversation with Cordelia (Charisma Carpenter) at the end of the episode, Angel acknowledges the evil in his nature by telling her, "It's still in me." Cordelia replies, giving voice to one of the themes of the series, "It's not the only thing in you."[7] Angel is still a vampire and has to constantly fight his evil nature, but he has the potential to do good, and the religious symbols help to develop that theme.

Like *Buffy*, *Angel* is primarily postmodern, validating multiple worldviews at once and showing skepticism toward any grand narratives that might unify the world. But certainly it explores religion deeply. In the episode "Dear Boy," Angel's maker and sometime lover tells him, "No matter how good a boy you are, God doesn't want you . . . But I still do."[8] Because these words are spoken by an untrustworthy character, it is not clear whether they are true or not—and the series never attempts a solid answer.

One of the most interesting plot arcs of the series is the one with Jasmine (Gina Torres), a beautiful anti-Christ figure who is miraculously born in corporeal form from Cordelia and Connor (Angel's romantic interest and his son, played by Vincent Kartheiser, also miraculously born from two vampires). Jasmine, a rogue member of the Powers That Be, brainwashes all those who come into contact with her into being perfectly happy, ignoring the pain and suffering in the world and thinking that everything is wonderful. It is only by being exposed to Jasmine's blood that individuals find their free will again and can recognize that Jasmine is not the embodiment of perfection they believed but rather a force intent on taking over the world through mind control.

Heralded by "The Beast" and biblical signs of an impending apocalypse, Jasmine speaks in language that is reminiscent of Jesus. She says things like, "With my help, all things are possible"[9] and "My love is all around you."[10] But her message is a completely amoral one. She tells Angel, "No. No, Angel. There are no absolutes. No right and wrong. Haven't you learned anything working for the Powers? There are only choices. I offered paradise. You chose this!"[11] The conclusion that Angel comes to is that individual free will is ultimately a priority, even if it leads to a suffering world. As a vampire with a soul, he is the individual most equipped to know that—as he has to fight every moment to do good in spite of his vampire nature, which constantly threatens to pull him into evil. He suffers because of it, but—as he tells Jasmine—it is worth the price.

Another characteristic of these shows is the way both vampires use their particular gifts and skills—part of their nature as a vampire—to do good. Knight uses his vampire skills of extraordinary senses, levitation/flying, and supernatural speed to catch criminals. And Angel uses his fighting abilities, strength, and speed for the same purposes. While certainly both characters face challenges based on their vampire natures (for instance, both are tempted around human blood, which makes it difficult for them to aid bleeding victims), they are still able to transform their natures into something that can do active good. In neither show is this atonement definite or conclusive. The series *Angel* ends without a resolution—the last shot is of Angel and his friends getting ready to fight yet another hopeless battle. The implication is that Angel's struggle for redemption is an eternal one. It doesn't have an end or an answer.

Similarly, *Forever Knight* ended, rather controversially, without a definite conclusion. After taking too much blood from his love, Natalie, Knight is faced with the decision of whether to let her die or bring her over as a vampire. He says he won't make her a vampire and asks LaCroix to kill him. The final shot is of LaCroix saying, "Damn you,"[12] but it isn't clear whether he carries through with Knight's death or not. Although both Angel and Knight are able to exert their free will and use their vampire skills to do good instead of evil, there isn't clear redemption for either one of them. Both shows conclude with the more traditional portrait of the vampire, which is one of a nature that damns them. But there remains in them the potential to do good, which turns vampires into a kind of hero.

Vampire Romances

Our culture seems to love a vampire romance, despite how bizarre the concept might be. The idea of a love scene—much less a long-term relationship—between a human and an animated corpse who feeds on human blood should raise eyebrows at the very least. But it no longer does. In order to place the vampire into a satisfying romance, the vampire must be transformed from its traditional portrayal. At the very least, it must not be evil. In vampire romance novels—which often maintain the traditional romance formula—the figure of the vampire must be sanitized or domesticated enough that he becomes a plausible hero, much in the way Meyer did in the Twilight Saga. There are less traditional romantic narratives that do not sanitize the vampire to such an extent, although the vampire must still remain sympathetic for the romance to work. We can see examples of these two patterns by looking briefly at popular paranormal romance writer Sherrilyn Kenyon and the recent Swedish film *Let the Right One In*, called by many critics the best vampire film ever made.

Sherrilyn Kenyon was one of the first romance authors to write in the now-booming genre of paranormal romance. Although Kenyon writes about a variety of paranormal beings, her Dark Hunters series is a good example of vampire fiction molded to fit the traditional romantic pattern. This pattern features a desirable alpha-hero—strong, handsome, powerful, successful, mysterious, and often emotionally scarred enough to make him hesitant about long-term relationships. In *Night Pleasures*, the first of her Dark Hunter series, Kenyon's hero is Kyrian of Thrace, an immortal "Dark Hunter." He fits all of the characteristics of a normal alpha-hero—desirability, power, and mystery. When Amanda, the heroine of the novel, first encounters him, she responds immediately to his desirability: "The heat of him warmed her and that raw, masculine aura of power overwhelmed her. . . . She wanted this man."[13] The only difficulty here is that Kyrian is not in fact a man. He is a vampire.

The typical romance formula is based on a conflict between the hero and heroine—a conflict that is strong enough to keep the two characters apart until it is overcome as they are reconciled in love. The conflict in *Night Pleasures* and many other vampire romances is prompted by the fact that the hero is not human—his nature is essentially different from the (usually) human heroine. While the heroine might have her own gifts—Amanda in *Night Pleasures* has the supernatural gift of prophetic dreams—usually the male hero is the vampire. In order for a romance to be effective, the readers must identify with the heroine and look at the hero as an object of desire. The hero's being a vampire causes an obvious conflict: how can a romance between a human woman and a vampire be successful? Kenyon makes use of this conflict. When Amanda realizes that Kyrian is a vampire, she immediately recognizes the difficulties: "*Mr. 'Do Me' Gorgeous Man is a vampire!* 'Oh no, no, no.' Amanda's entire body shook from terror and it took every piece of self-control she possessed not to launch into a screaming fit. 'Are you going to suck my blood?'"[14] As anyone can recognize, there are some inevitable problems in a potential romance between a human and a creature whose instinct would always be to feed on her.

In order to make the romance work, the nature of the traditional vampire has to be significantly altered. Just as Edward and the other Cullens in the Twilight saga were made to be "good" vampires, so the heroes of other vampire romances are made good rather than evil, often without even the moral tension we see in characters like Angel and Knight. In Kenyon's fictional world, Dark Hunters are not normal vampires. They have fangs, they can only go out at night, they have lost their souls, and they are immortal. But their role is to hunt other vampires—those vampires that seek to do harm. When Amanda asks Kyrian the difference between a Dark Hunter and a vampire, he tells her, "The difference is I don't normally kill humans . . ."[15] Kenyon has created an entire backstory and mythology for the existence of Dark Hunters and other immortals, but the mythology is primarily in service of creating a sanitized vampire—a character with the dark mystery and power of the vampire but without any of the inconvenient habits, like blood drinking.

The conflict between the hero and heroine in *Night Pleasure*—the issues keeping Amanda and Kyrian apart—is not simply his immortal nature. The relationship is also complicated by both characters' past relationships and also by Kyrian's belief that he is supposed to be alone. Dark Hunters are "reborn to walk alone through time,"[16] which makes long-term romantic relationships a problem for them. Thus, in order for the romance to have a happy ending, Kyrian's very nature must change. In the mythology Kenyon creates, a change in nature is possible. Kyrian can and does become a human again, so he and Amanda can have a life together as a couple.

The "vampire" characteristics Kenyon gives to her hero are almost entirely superficial. The fangs are explained as "part and parcel" of the animal characteristics given to Dark Hunters in order to track the Daimons they hunt.[17] Although Kyrian claims at one point to have to struggle against "sinking [his] teeth into [Amanda's] neck" whenever they are close,[18] nothing else in the novel actually supports this claim. Kyrian never really struggles with his vampire nature the way Edward does in the Twilight saga and Bill does in the Southern Vampire Mysteries. Kenyon uses many of the features of a vampire primarily for atmosphere and to intensify the mystery and power of her alpha-hero. The prologue ends with a rather clichéd description of the Dark Hunter: "He is Solitude. He is Darkness. He is the shadow in the night . . . until he can find the one woman who will not betray him. The one pure heart who can see past his dark side and bring him back into the light."[19] Kyrian is not actually dark or dangerous in the novel. He is an attractive, powerful man who is not significantly different from human heroes in hundreds of other romance novels. While it is certainly possible to develop a romantic relationship while still genuinely exploring the themes traditionally connected to the figure of the vampire, the pairings that do this most effectively—like Buffy and Angel in *Buffy the Vampire Slayer*—are inevitably doomed.

Let the Right One In is a film released in 2008, directed by Tomas Alfredson and based on a book of the same name by John Ajvide Lindqvist. The film highlights the romance between the two main characters—a bullied twelve-year-old boy and a vampire child—more than the horror aspects present in the book. The film tells the story of Oskar (Kåre Hedebrant), a socially isolated boy who is constantly bullied at school and is emotionally distant from his divorced parents. He channels his angst into playing at revenge against those who have hurt him. He is attacking a tree at night outside of his apartment building—telling it to "Squeal like a pig"—when he first meets Eli.[20] A female actress plays Eli (Lina Leandersson), and Oskar believes she is a girl, even though she tells him she is not. In the book, Eli is a boy who was castrated by a vampire, but the film never makes that explicit. Despite the gender ambiguity, the romance develops at the beginning of the film in predictable ways, with initial conflict (both telling the other to go home) transforming into bonding over a Rubik's Cube and shared candy, although the candy makes Eli sick. Eli is a vampire, and she lives with an adult man who kills and drains the blood out of people in order to feed her. Later in the film, the man burns himself with acid just before he is caught murdering someone so he won't be recognized and thus connected to Eli. Eli comes to him in the hospital and accepts his offer for her to feed from him, killing him in the process.

The vampire nature in the film is neither sanitized nor eroticized. The filming does not gloss over the more disgusting aspects of Eli's feeding—including sounds and blood smeared all over her face and shirt. In one scene, when Oskar cuts his hands so he and Eli can mix their blood, sealing their relationship, Eli ravenously licks his blood off the floor and then has to flee in order to not attack him. The real conflict comes after Oskar realizes she is a vampire—she admits that she lives on blood, although she claims she is not dead. With the narrative subtlety of the rest of the film, Oskar pulls away from Eli, to the point where he teases her into entering his home without an invitation—which causes Eli to bleed from the eyes and skin. Oskar is horrified by the consequence of his petty behavior and invites her in quickly, hugging her. Then Eli tells him that she is "like" him. When Oskar says that *he* doesn't murder people, she says that he would if he could, out of revenge. She says, "I do it because I have to. Be me for a while."[21] This is the moment of true connection for them, when Oskar realizes that Eli is in fact not significantly different than he is, even though she is a vampire and kills people to feed.

153

The film concludes with an affirmation of this connection and the similarity between them. Oskar saves Eli from a man who is about to let the sunlight into the room where she is sleeping. Then he shuts the door while she kills and feeds off the man. Afterward they kiss despite her bloody mouth. She says she needs to leave and appears to do so. But then, when the school bullies persecute Oskar at a swimming pool, holding him under water, Eli comes back and kills the bullies for him. The last scene shows Oskar on a train next to a trunk. When the knocking of Morse Code comes from the trunk (tapping out the word "Kiss"), it is clear that Eli is in the trunk. Despite the fact that the film does not sanitize vampires, it does humanize them. Or rather, it explores the way Eli as a vampire is really no different than Oskar as a human child. Their romance succeeds because at heart they are the same. The film also explores the moral ambiguity we saw in some other vampire stories—where vampires inevitably have a different moral standard than humans do.

In these two quite different examples, we can see that—in order to make an effective vampire love story—the vampire must become sympathetic and show himself or herself to have a nature like the one they love. That happens in Kenyon by turning the vampire into a traditional hero and in *Let the Right One In* by developing the concept that humans are really no better than vampires—everyone is working by moral standards that are not traditional notions of right and wrong.

Metaphysical Power and the Sexy Vampire

The sexy vampire is so common in contemporary popular culture that it has become a cliché. We can certainly see female versions of a beautiful, desirable vampire—like Salma Hayek's character in the film *From Dusk Till Dawn*, doing her provocative erotic dance with an albino snake. But more commonly, particularly within the genre of paranormal fiction, the sexually desirable vampire is male. Sometimes these take the form of vampire romance like Kenyon's. Another trend, however, is to alter the typical romantic pattern and make the vampire a desirable sex partner but not a traditional romantic mate in a long-term, monogamous relationship. Harris fits this second pattern in the way she handles both Bill and Eric in the Southern Vampire Mysteries. This trend is also exemplified by Laurel K. Hamilton in her Anita Blake, Vampire Hunter series.

This pattern uses the sex appeal of the vampire but creates a more plausible vampire characterization. Because vampires are associated with genuine power and danger, they cannot be easy romantic partners. Like in Harris's novels, Hamilton's novels pose vampires as possibilities for either short-term or nonmonogamous relationships with great sex, but not necessarily for committed, monogamous relationships. Hamilton's Anita Blake series is one of the earliest examples of paranormal fiction and urban fantasy, and it inspired much of the fiction in those genres that followed. In *Guilty Pleasures*, the first novel of the series, we meet Anita Blake, the central character. She is an "animator." Her job is to raise the dead as zombies. She also works for the police as a consultant about supernatural matters, and she kills vampires or other preternatural creatures when an official warrant is issued for their execution.

Vampires in the novels are not sanitized or domesticated the way they are in Kenyon's novels. They maintain the depth of power and danger that they traditionally possess in vampire lore. They are not all entirely evil, although many of them are. Hamilton uses the figure of the vampire to explore power more than sin—so she has certainly moved away from the themes of *Dracula*. But in her fictional world, vampires are not and can never be perfectly safe or familiar or comfortable—even when Anita is in intimate relationships with them. In *Guilty Pleasures*, the master vampire and chief villain is in the body of a little girl. Nikolaos is described as "looking ethereal and lovely like a painting."[22] But when her mind is opened to Anita, the power is overwhelming:

> Her mind crashed against mine and I staggered. Thoughts ripped into me like knives, steel-edged dreams. Fleeting bits of her mind danced in my head; where they touched I was numbed, hurt.
>
> I was on my knees, and I didn't remember falling. I was cold, so cold. There was nothing for me. I was an insignificant thing, beside that mind. How could I think to call myself an equal? How could I do anything but crawl to her and beg to be forgiven? My insolence was intolerable.[23]

While not inherently evil, there is nothing easy, safe, or domesticated about the vampires in Hamilton's novels. If a vampire is old and powerful enough, he cannot safely be killed, even during the day.

Guilty Pleasures ends with Anita admitting she is drawn to the beautiful, desirable vampire Jean-Claude but concluding, "I know who and what I am. I am The Executioner, and I don't date vampires. I kill them."[24] Of course, her determination to avoid dating vampires does not last. In the later books, as Anita becomes attracted to more than one vampire (and shape-shifter as well) and enters into relationships with them, they still are too deep, powerful, and unknowable to be typical romantic partners. She eventually becomes Jean-Claude's "consort," but their relationship is never monogamous.

The resistance to monogamy has a number of causes, but the primary reason is Anita's gaining of the *ardeur* from

Jean-Claude. The *ardeur* is a supernatural, primal hunger that requires her to feed on lust daily. As she grows to understand it more, she realizes that the *ardeur* makes her a kind of living vampire. Just as vampires feed on blood to survive, so Anita feeds on lust (and anger, as some of the later novels explore). Anita's increasingly complicated love life must accommodate her needs and the needs of all of her partners—some vampire, some shape-shifter, all with particular and sometimes contradictory needs from their natures, their preternatural politics, and their own personalities. In *Cerulean Sins*, Anita is in a sexual relationship with Jean-Claude. But Asher, another vampire, becomes a third in their bed—in part to protect him from the master vampire Belle Morte. Anita is also in a relationship with Micah, a wereleopard, and several other characters. In one sense, the mythology seems to be in service to working as much sex as possible into the narrative. On another level, Hamilton does use sex for thematic purposes. It is part of her exploration of power. There is as much intimacy in the supernatural connections between the characters—including the vampire exchange of blood—as there is in actual sex acts.

This connection between vampires, metaphysical power, and sex leads to some very gray situations and narrative devices, many involving nonconsensual sex. Anita's *ardeur* overtakes her free will in driving her to have sex even when she would choose not to do so. And it also affects the men around her, so they are driven to have sex against their free will as well. There are other potentially nonconsensual situations—as in *Skin Trade*, where the chief villain, a vampire named Vittorio, holds people hostage and forces Anita to engage in sexual activity, which is eroticized by the narrative. In two of the latest novels, *Blood Noir* and *Skin Trade*, Anita is possessed by Marmee Noir, one of the most ancient vampires in existence. Marmee Noir is an overwhelming power and darkness and tries to use Anita's body to awaken from a one-thousand-year sleep. She needs power from the *ardeur* to do so, so she takes over Anita's body and leads her to a kind of group orgy in both cases, with Anita having sex with multiple partners. The nonconsensual behavior is usually eroticized, and—although Anita struggles emotionally afterward, at least to a certain extent—Hamilton never genuinely examines the issue seriously. This is one of the consequences of conflating sex, metaphysical power, and vampire characteristics as Hamilton does. Anita gets mind raped and physically raped more than once in the novels, and she does the same thing to the men around her (usually unintentionally). But because it is always explained as a metaphysical necessity, it is not taken for the serious issue it is.

This overlap between sex, blood, and magic power exchanges is a primary feature of Hamilton's novels. And ultimately it serves her major theme—which is power rather than sin. Anita, more and more, wonders if she is becoming a monster as she loses her sense of morality and kills more and more creatures. While she occasionally feels bad about the change, her conclusions (sometimes unspoken) are always that this change in attitude is necessary for her to survive and do her job. In *The Harlequin*, Anita tells the vampire leader of the Church of Eternal Life (a church for vampires), "Free will is for humans, Malcolm. The preternatural community is about control."[25] Although Hamilton keeps certain aspects of the vampire tradition, including the power of the cross when it is wielded by someone who has genuine Christian faith (like Anita), her ultimate purpose is secular rather than theological. Just as the concept of sin is transformed into vampire communities' own systems of right and wrong, so Hamilton develops the concept of vampire power that takes on a life of its own. Morality is no longer at issue, and the power can be used to save as much as to destroy.

In order to make vampires sympathetic, the traditional vampire mythology must be transformed. In shows like *Forever Knight* and *Angel*, the vampires repent of the evil their vampire natures led them to and seek to do good in endless pursuit of redemption. In vampire romances, a satisfying conclusion is only possible when the vampire becomes humanized—either by domesticating the portrait of the vampire or by showing little difference between vampire nature and human nature. And in paranormal fiction like Hamilton's, vampires do not have to become "good guys" in order to be sympathetic heroes. No one is really good in a world that is all about power. While the vampires in these stories can certainly be dangerous, they are no more dangerous than anyone else. So either humans have become monsters or the vampire has lost its fangs.

Conclusion

> Be me for a while.
>
> The vampire Eli in *Let the Right One In*

Vampires matter to us. They are not significant to us—at least, not to contemporary culture in a broad sense—in their "literal" manifestation. For the most part, we don't worry about our neighbors and co-workers extending their fangs and sinking them into our necks, and we don't go through elaborate rituals involving garlic and wild rose to keep the bodies of our loved ones in their graves at night. Rather, vampires matter to us as metaphors, in what they represent. We can see in them parts of ourselves—our darkest fears or our deepest desires. The evidence of their significance is in a long, varied history of vampire lore, literature, film, and television.

God created us as humans with an innate attraction to symbols. We can see this played out in the way we use the Christian cross, the bread and wine of the Lord's Supper, and the water of baptism. But our need for symbols extends beyond our religious lives. We keep returning in the Western tradition to vampires because, in the vampire, we find a symbol that allows us to tell the stories we need to tell.

Like all traditional symbols or metaphors, the figure of the vampire has morphed as the culture that produces it has changed. One of the things that has made the vampire such a powerful metaphor is the spiritual and theological potential it holds. The vampire allowed us to explore the concepts of temptation, sin, and guilt. The vampire provided a means to express the need for redemption, the power of faith, and the necessity of sacrifice. The vampire gave us a creative space to understand the fight against evil, spiritual warfare, and what it means for something to be sacred. Few vampire stories have done all of these things, but the metaphor is rich and layered enough to make such exploration possible. As the figure of the vampire in contemporary culture becomes increasingly secular, the spiritual and theological potential in the vampire is gradually being lost.

Christians have let this happen. Part of this is because some are threatened by vampire literature and think it must be dark, demonic, or associated with the occult. While the figure of the vampire certainly can be associated with those things, the previous chapters have shown many ways in which the vampire can in fact affirm a Christian worldview. Another reason Christians have failed to reclaim the metaphor of the vampire is because of apathy. If vampires are simply one of many bizarre, inane cultural fads, perhaps they are not worth considering thoughtfully and reflecting on from a Christian perspective. But vampires are not simply a fad. They are deeply rooted in the Western tradition. And although the heights of popularity they have reached recently will likely be replaced by a new figure or feature of a best-selling novel, vampires in literature, film, and television—in the stories we tell ourselves—are not likely to go away.

As Christians, we believe that God has revealed himself to us in written text, in the Bible. Because of this, one of the most important skills we can cultivate is the ability to read well. We shouldn't just read the Bible well. We should also read human expressions of themselves—the stories we tell, the metaphors we value, the various articulations of the way we understand ourselves and the world. This means reading carefully and reading deeply. It means informed reading—understanding and taking into consideration such things as context, genre, and audience. It means valuing the text itself and using it to understand more about the world God created and who we are as humans, sinful but made in God's image. Vampires are not irrelevant. They can't be. Because they tell us something about ourselves.

Christians who believe this and genuinely want to understand and engage with our culture sometimes have the tendency to jump on the cultural bandwagon, without thinking through the significance of what they are interacting with or using a worldview founded in God's truth to understand it. While the vampire genre has a lot of potential for theological reflection from Christian writers and artists, it is not likely to be done by trying to write another *Twilight* or Southern Vampire Mystery. While those stories are certainly worth examining and understanding—even appreciating—the secularization of the vampire in those stories does not allow as much opportunity for Christian expression. But there are plenty of examples in the vampire tradition to inspire a Christian's creativity. We can look to *Dracula* for an example of how the vampire allows for an exploration of sin and temptation and the Christian as spiritual warrior. We can see in Anne Rice's novels a picture of the baffling and elusive relationship between the flesh and the spirit, which leads to real theological questions that are well worth asking. We can find

163

in the character of Angel on *Buffy the Vampire Slayer* and its spin-off *Angel* an embodiment of the consequences of sin without the grace to be found in the work of Jesus Christ.

The vampire can engage both the intellect and the imagination of the Christian, but it is not likely to happen by accident. Using the vampire to explore human experience that is not spiritual or theological is certainly not bad in and of itself, and we shouldn't devalue those stories that do so. But it is worth recognizing that, as the vampire figure has lost its spiritual potency, it has lost much of its metaphorical power. If the vampire represents for us aspects of ourselves that make us human, then the spiritual and theological aspects are necessary for a fuller, richer picture. If Christians can understand the vampire better, we can discuss, create, and inspire a respiritualized figure of the vampire. In doing so, we can help return the vampire tradition to the power it once had.

We can give vampires their fangs again.

Timeline of Referenced Vampire Texts

1816   Coleridge's "Christabel," poem
1819   Polidori's *The Vampyre*, story
1845   *Varney the Vampire*, serialized story, published through 1847
1872   Le Fanu's *Carmilla*, story
1897   Stoker's *Dracula*, novel
1931   *Dracula*, film
1936   *Dracula's Daughter*, film
1943   *Son of Dracula*, film
1945   *House of Dracula*, film
1973   Character of Blade first appeared in Marvel comic "The Tomb of Dracula"
1976   Rice's *Interview with the Vampire*, novel (the Vampire Chronicles series continued through 2003)
1978   Yarbro's *Hôtel Transylvania*, novel (Saint-Germain series continues as of 2010)
1983   Kikuchi's *Vampire Hunter D*, first novel of series
1985   *Vampire Hunter D*, animated film

1992   *Buffy the Vampire Slayer*, film

1992   *Forever Knight*, television program (first episodes adapted from 1989 television movie, series aired through 1996)

1993   Hamilton's *Guilty Pleasures*, novel (Anita Blake series continues as of 2010)

1994   *Interview with the Vampire*, film

1996   *From Dusk Till Dawn*, film

1996   *Kindred: The Embraced*, television series

1997   *Buffy the Vampire Slayer*, television series, aired through 2003

1998   *Blade*, film (sequels follow in 2002 and 2004)

1999   *Angel*, television series, aired through 2004

2001   Harris's *Dead Until Dark*, novel (the Southern Vampire Mysteries series continues as of 2010)

2002   Kenyon's *Night Pleasures* (Dark Hunter series continues as of 2010)

2003   *Underworld*, film (sequels follow in 2006 and 2009)

2004   Lindqvist's *Let the Right One In*, novel

2005   Meyer's *Twilight*, novel (the Twilight Saga continued through 2008)

2008   *True Blood*, television series (still aired as of 2010)

2008   *Let the Right One In*, film

2008   *Twilight*, film (films based on the books continue as of 2011)

Notes

Chapter 1: Why Vampires Matter

1. Auerbach, *Our Vampires, Ourselves*, 145.

2. For instance, Laurence A. Rickels's *Vampire Lectures* uses Freudian theory to analyze the vampire from its earliest appearance in nineteenth-century fiction to contemporary television shows like *Buffy the Vampire Slayer*. Other scholars like Ken Gelder and Nina Auerbach explore the topic through a cultural or sociopolitical lens and argue that the image of the vampire has become an embodiment of a culture or time period's central concerns. And Joan Gordon and Veronica Hollinger's *Blood Read* focuses on the vampire as a metaphor in popular culture, each essay exploring a different metaphorical manifestation.

3. "First Taste," *True Blood*, 1.2.

Chapter 2: Bram Stoker's *Dracula*

1. Stoker, *Dracula*, 31.

2. Readers and critics don't just overlook the distinct significance of the cross. They also take the religious aspects of the novel completely for granted. Because the Christian elements are so dominant and so fundamental to the novel, the absence of critical examination of them is both noteworthy and problematic. Among the few articles that consider religion in an intentional way is Christopher Gist Raible's "Dracula: Christian Heretic," a brief article that argues that the novel is a "morality play" (105) but that it consistently inverts or perverts Christian truths. While

not specifically handling the Christian content of the novel, Gwyneth Hood does focus on some of its biblical and religious themes in her article "Sauron and Dracula," in which she compares Tolkien's and Stoker's Satanic heroes. Otherwise, the few in-depth examinations of the Christian elements of *Dracula* can be found in articles that are focused more on the film adaptations than on the novel itself, like Jacque Coulardeau's "The Vision of Religion in Francis Ford Coppola's *Bram Stoker's Dracula*" (2007) and Stephenson Humphries-Brooks's "The Body and the Blood of Eternal UnDeath" (2004).

Not only are the religious aspects of the novel often overlooked in favor of trendier topics of criticism, but Bram Stoker's religious life is also often generally overlooked in biographies. He was an Irish Protestant rather than a Catholic, and so religion was certainly important in his life in terms of his nationality and social standing. But the biographies of Stoker focus primarily on his career, his relationships, his early childhood illness, and his interest in mesmerism and other occult practices in order to draw connections between his life and *Dracula*—rather than any of his religious or spiritual experiences. During his lifetime, he was better known for his part in the career of the actor Henry Irving (the first man to be knighted for acting in England) than for his work as a writer. He was the business manager of the Lyceum Theatre in London for a good portion of his professional career, and his most famous work during his lifetime was his 700-page *Personal Reminiscences of Henry Irving* (1906). Any individual commitment he had to religious faith, other than his church affiliation, is not well-documented, so we must look to the novel itself for evidence of the Christian worldview it affirms.

3. One of the dominant lines of scholarly treatment of *Dracula* focuses on unveiling the historical and folk influences on the story and characters. The earliest academic study of *Dracula* was not published until 1956, with Bacil Kirtley's article, "*Dracula*, the Monastic Chronicles and Slavic Folklore," in which the author explores Stoker's sources in folklore and cultural tradition. Kirtley was one of the first to expound on the history of the Romanian Vlad the Impaler as a chief inspiration for the story. This thesis was further developed later with Grigore Nandris's "The Historical Dracula" (1966), and it reached a wider audience in the 1972 book-length study by McNally and Florescu, *In Search of Dracula*. McNally and Florescu include discussion of the Hungarian "Blood Countess," Elisabeth Bathory, who is believed to have murdered hundreds of peasant girls and bathed in their blood. Gabriel Ronay in *The Truth about Dracula* (1972) claims that Stoker must have been more influenced by the Countess than by Vlad himself. Many scholars doubt the plausibility of this connection, however. This kind of criticism continues even still, with articles like

Marius Crişan's "The Models for Castle Dracula in Stoker's Sources on Transylvania," published in 2008. In these kinds of critical treatments, the features and the significance of the novel are opened up by connecting the events and setting with historical or cultural inspirations. Often, they focus less on the worldview presented in the novel than they do the sometimes peripheral textual features, but they are certainly helpful for better understanding the novel and Stoker's purposes.

4. Stoker, *Dracula*, 52.

5. In addition to digging into the folk and historical influences on *Dracula*, the two other major lines of criticism applied to the novel today are psychoanalytic criticism and postcolonial and Irish studies. In 1959, Maurice Richardson did a psychoanalytic study of *Dracula*, arguing that the Freudian perspective is the only one that can be successfully applied to Stoker's work. In a notorious and often-quoted passage, Richardson calls *Dracula* "a kind of incestuous necrophilous, oral-anal-sadistic all-in wrestling match" that is set in "a sort of homicidal lunatic's brothel in a crypt" (427). Other important psychological studies of the novel include Leonard Wolf's Jungian *A Dream of Dracula* (1972) and Joseph Bierman's "Dracula: Prolonged Childhood Illness and the Oral Triad" (also 1972), which explores the novel from the perspective of Stoker's own psychology. These psychoanalytic studies were followed by a whole collection of psychosexual readings—including those by Phyllis A. Roth, Judith Weissman, Gail B. Griffin, Christopher Bentley, Thomas B. Byers, Christopher Craft, and John Allen Stevenson—which continues to be one of the most often-used critical lenses for examining the novel. Often combined with the psychosexual perspective are gender studies of *Dracula*, and Stoker's portrayal of women continues to be one of the most popular aspects of the novel for scholars to explore. It's difficult to argue against the rich potential for psychoanalytical and psychosexual readings of the novel, but the overwhelming focus on this perspective has limited our understanding of *Dracula* to merely one level.

The most popular recent trend in criticism is postcolonial and Irish studies of the novel, focusing on how Stoker uses ideas connected to the history of the British Empire and the treatment of the Irish to develop his characters and themes. These examinations include Stephen Arata's "The Occidental Tourist: *Dracula* and the Anxiety of Reverse Colonization" (1990) and Cannon Schmitt's "Mother Dracula: Orientalism, Degeneration, and the Anglo-Irish National Subjectivity at the Fin de Siècle" (1994). The Irish perspective is argued convincingly by Michael Valdez Moses in "The Irish Vampire: *Dracula*, Parnell and the Troubled Dreams of Nationhood" (1997). These studies are a welcome change from the heavily psychoanalytic emphasis until recently, and they open up new levels of inquiry in regard to Stoker's fiction and its significance to larger issues of politics, nationality, ethnicity, and social justice.

6. Stoker, *Dracula*, 36.

7. Ibid., 41–42.

8. Ibid., 45.

9. Ibid., 46.

10. Ibid., 46.

11. Ibid., 50.

12. Ibid., 62.

13. Ibid., 73.

14. Ibid., 61–62.

15. Ibid., 62.

16. Ibid., 52.

17. Ibid., 48.

18. Ibid., 75.

19. Ibid., 80.

20. For instance, the description of Lucy in the coffin writhing, with "opened red lips" and "wild contortions" until Arthur thrusts the phallic stake into her body is quite rightly read by most critics as having sexual connotations. Stoker, *Dracula*, 223.

21. Stoker, *Dracula*, 117.

22. We can see a similar focus on the soul, the spiritual, in R. M. Renfield, the "zoophagus" eater of life in the form of flies, spiders, and birds. In one of his brief bouts of sanity, when he is able to shake free of Dracula's influence, he implores Dr. Seward to let him go so he can no longer be a tool of Dracula's. He begs in a beautifully rhythmic passage: "By all you hold sacred—by all you hold dear—by your love that is lost—by your hope that lives—for the sake of the Almighty, take me out of this and save my soul from guilt! Can't you hear me, man? Can't you understand? Will you never learn? Don't you know that I am sane and earnest now; that I am no lunatic in a mad fit, but a sane man fighting for his soul" (251). The entire experience with vampires, from both the victims and the Christian warriors, is posed in spiritual terms.

23. Stoker, *Dracula*, 221–24.

24. Ibid., 155.

25. Ibid., 221–22.

26. Ibid., 271.

27. Ibid., 280.

28. Ibid., 242.

29. For the purposes of the novel, I think we are supposed to believe that Van Helsing has permission to use the sacramental wafers as he does, although most agree that Stoker is stretching credibility at this point by

implying the Roman Catholic Church would have allowed such a thing. Some readers have argued that Van Helsing must be lying because of the unlikelihood of his claim, but I see nothing in the novel to support such a reading. Van Helsing, throughout, is portrayed as a sincerely devout Christian warrior, and his lying about permission to use the Host is not a particularly convincing reading.

30. Stoker, *Dracula*, 285.

31. Ibid., 296.

32. Ibid.

33. Ibid., 316.

34. Ibid., 201.

35. Ibid., 202.

36. Ibid., 350.

37. Ibid., 353.

38. Ibid., 368.

39. The popular online study guide *SparkNotes*, for instance, claims the use of Christian symbolism makes the novel read like a work of religious propaganda ("Sparknote on *Dracula*," 2003, www.sparknotes.com/lit/dracula/themes.html).

Chapter 3: Anne Rice's Vampire Chronicles

1. Riley, *Conversations with Anne Rice*, 145.

2. Ibid., 159.

3. The dates of her return to the church and the commitment of her writing to Christ are those specified on her official website, AnneRice .com: http://www.annerice.com/Chamber-Biography.html. The public announcement of her rejection of Christianity was made on her Facebook page in two different posts on July 28, 2010 (http://www.facebook.com/annericefanpage). In the weeks that followed, in a number of online, print, television, and radio interviews, she consistently used the language "quitting Christianity in the name of Christ" to describe her rejection of organized religion.

4. Lloyd Worley argues that the vampire's lack of fear of religious objects reflects modern culture's rejection of Catholic tradition and thus Rice's vampires are "Protestant in religion, existentialist in outlook, and absurd in ethic" ("Anne Rice's Protestant Vampires," 80), but—aside from the lack of reverence for religious objects—her vampires have very little of a Protestant worldview or sensibility.

5. Martin Wood has a helpful essay on the various ways Rice challenges the vampire tradition by forcing readers to "confront the core truths of the myth itself" ("New Life for an Old Tradition: Anne Rice and Vampire Literature," 59).

6. More than one critic has explored Rice's moral and spiritual ideas in the Vampire Chronicles. Kathleen Rout, in "Who Do You Love? Anne Rice's Vampires and Their Moral Transition," notes the shift in Rice's morality over the years in which she wrote the Chronicles—changing from the "moral neutrality" of the first few novels to a "non-violent endorsement of global peace between vampires and human beings" (473). Edward J. Ingebretsen reads Rice's *Interview with the Vampire* in the tradition of the "theologized gothic" ("Anne Rice: Raising Holy Hell, Harlequin Style," 93), and Aileen Chris Shafer explores the moral ambiguity in *The Vampire Lestat* ("Let Us Prey: Religious Codes and Ritual in *The Vampire Lestat*"). Terri R Liberman also tackles the issue of morality in the Chronicles in "Eroticism as Moral Fulcrum in Rice's Vampire Chronicles," in which she claims that Rice challenges moral taboos through her choice of erotic objects in the novels, and in doing so implies that "morality must be defined anew" (109).

7. Katherine Ramsland, in *Prism of the Night*, uses a quote from Rice's husband, Stan Rice, about the parallel imaginative course he and his wife took in response to their daughter's death: "The history of a blood disease led into images of the vampire and in my work . . . the idea of the lamb that is sacrificed, the blood of the lamb. We started out in different places, but a lot of our ideas came together" (167).

8. Ramsland talks about how stimulating Rice found the mysteries of church sacraments, particularly transubstantiation, as a teenager. Ramsland continues by explaining how Rice felt "sexual stirrings" at the religious images confronting her (*Prism of the Night*, 30), and as "a result of the excitement and dread of participating in the forbidden, and anticipating possible punishment, she had sexual fantasies with a masochistic flavor" (31). This conflating of religious and sexual influences is sometimes evident in the Vampire Chronicles.

9. Rice, *Interview with the Vampire*, 6.

10. Ibid., 15.

11. Ibid., 65.

12. Ibid., 130.

13. Ibid., 131.

14. Ibid., 146.

15. A continuing motif throughout the Vampire Chronicles is found in moments of confrontation between the vampire and a human woman who is suddenly made aware of the vampire's true nature. We see this begin with Louis's confrontation with Babette, who exclaims, "Get thee behind me, Satan" (*Interview with the Vampire*, 61). This confrontation is mirrored in *Tale of the Body Thief* when Lestat confronts Gretchen, who either has a psychological collapse or a spiritual transformation from the

shock of the revelation, and again with Lestat's confrontation in *Memnoch the Devil* with Dora, who manages to see beyond Lestat's vampire nature and believe in some good from his existence and presence in her life. All of these moments of revelation and confrontation highlight the spiritual torment underlying the condition of being a vampire.

16. Rice, *Interview with the Vampire*, 214.

17. Ibid., 257.

18. As an example of another vampire who reaches a similar conclusion about the lack of place and purpose for vampire existence, Marius summarizes his conclusions—very similar to Louis's—about the same question in *The Vampire Lestat*. He says to Lestat, "What can I say finally that will not confirm your worst fears? I have lived over eighteen hundred years, and I tell you life does not need us. I have never had a true purpose. We have no place" (466).

19. Rice, *Interview with the Vampire*, 303–5.

20. Rice quoted in Riley, *Conversations with Anne Rice*, 18.

21. Rice, *Vampire Lestat*, 31.

22. Ibid., 87.

23. Rice, *Tale of the Body Thief*, 68.

24. Rice, *Vampire Lestat*, 143.

25. Ibid., 383.

26. Ibid., 445.

27. Ibid., 459.

28. Rice, *Queen of the Damned*, 239.

29. Ibid., 273.

30. Ibid., 409.

31. Akasha seeks to impose her world order on others, preventing them from making free choices and deciding what is right for them. Her message is simply too narrow and simplistic to be good. As Lestat tells Akasha, "History is a litany of injustice, no one denies it. But when has a simple solution been anything but evil? Only in complexity do we find answers. Through complexity do men struggle toward fairness. It is slow and clumsy, but it's the only way. Simplicity demands too great a sacrifice. It always has" (*Queen of the Damned*, 407). This imposition of a simple answer on everyone—the answer Rice implies religions offer—is counter the "Savage Garden" philosophy, and thus must be resisted.

32. Rice quoted in Ramsland, *Vampire Companion*, 122, 460.

33. Roberts, *Anne Rice*, 58.

34. Rice, *Queen of the Damned*, 423.

35. Rice, *Interview with the Vampire*, 79.

36. Ibid., 128.

37. Rice, *Memnoch the Devil*, 79.

38. Ibid., 100.

39. Ibid., 157.

40. Ibid., 161.

41. Ibid., 169.

42. Ibid., 283.

43. See AnneRice.com, www.annerice.com/Bookshelf-Memnoch.html.

44. Rice, *Memnoch the Devil*, 335.

45. Ibid., 346.

46. Rice, *Blackwood Farm*, 77.

47. Rice, *Memnoch the Devil*, 353.

48. In *Blackwood Farm*, we have in Quinn Blackwood another vampire who, through his spiritual experiences, comes to an understanding of his theological nature and his place in the universe. In a lengthy, reflective passage, we can see Quinn working through all of the issues discussed in this chapter so far. And he too concludes with an emphasis on God's human face: "I thought of the omniscient God becoming Man and it seemed such a remarkable gesture! It was as if I'd never heard the story before! And it seemed that the omniscient God had to do it to fully understand His Creation because He had created something that could offend Him so deeply as humankind had done" (498). It is the incarnate God that moves Quinn so deeply, and his guilt feels absolved (at least momentarily) by an emotional, human connection with Christ.

Later in the novel, in an ironic turnaround, Lestat absolves Quinn of sin in the name of the Trinity. And then they have a somewhat traditional exorcism, calling on God to free Quinn of Goblin, the spirit who won't leave him alone. This act can be juxtaposed to the ceremony in *Merrick*, when Merrick tries to summon Claudia's ghost by calling on a variety of spiritual beings, not simply Christian ones. When the ceremony concludes, Quinn witnesses the Light and has a spiritually transcendent experience that Lestat is never able to have. The reason for this distinction is never clear, but each vampire has his own experience with God and spirituality. And all of the meaningful experiences are connected to the human face of God.

49. Rice quoted in Riley, *Conversations with Anne Rice*, 148.

50. Candace Benefiel's essay, "Blood Relations: The Gothic Perversion of the Nuclear Family in Anne Rice's *Interview with the Vampire*," effectively explores the concept of family in the depiction of Louis, Lestat, and Claudia.

51. Rice, *Interview with the Vampire*, 281.

52. Rice, *Vampire Armand*, 177.

53. Ibid., 299–300.

54. Ibid., 385.

55. Rice, *Blood Canticle*, 5.

56. In *Blood Canticle*, we have in Mona a new vampire who is trying to work through the same questions as Louis, Lestat, Armand, Marius, David Talbot, and Quinn. She does so through the meditation on her experiences as a newly born vampire that she is writing and sharing with Lestat. In her musings, she expresses some of the spiritual questions all of the other novels have explored: "How does God view my essential being? Am I human and vampire? Or vampire only? That is, is damnation, and I speak now not of literal Hell with flames, but of a state which is defined by the absence of God—is damnation implicit and inherent in what I am, or do I still exist in a relativistic universe in which I may attain grace on the same terms as humans can attain it, by participating in the Incarnation of Christ, an historical event in which I totally believe, in spite of the fact that it is not philosophically fashionable, though what questions of fashion have to do with me now in this transcendent and often luminous condition is moot" (99). Later she admits in those same mediations not to truly know the answer to the questions and admits that it is possible that her spiritual wanderings will never end.

57. Rice, *Blood Canticle*, 141.

58. Ibid., 260.

59. Ibid., 301.

60. Ibid., 306.

Chapter 4: *Buffy the Vampire Slayer*

1. "The Gift," *Buffy the Vampire Slayer*, 5.22.

2. Thus far, Jana Reiss's *What Would Buffy Do? The Vampire Slayer as Spiritual Guide* is the only book-length study of the show's spiritual themes, although the topic has been tackled in essays or book chapters from various points of view. Neal King's "Brownskirts: Fascism, Christianity, and the Eternal Demon" in *Buffy the Vampire Slayer and Philosophy* argues that the show's moral treatment—influenced by Christian tradition—is fascist and should be reconsidered. Matthew Pateman has a very interesting discussion of Buffy's relationship to the Christian conception of apocalypse and eschatology in his chapter "Aesthetics, Culture and History" in *The Aesthetics of Culture in Buffy the Vampire Slayer*. Wendy Love Anderson's excellent essay "Prophecy Girl and the Powers That Be: The Philosophy of Religion in the Buffyverse" claims that ultimately religion is subjugated to secondary importance in service of relationships and human experience.

3. For instance, in the first episode of season 7, "Lessons," The First appears to a guilt-ridden Spike and tells him that "It's not about right.

It's not about wrong. It's about power." But The First's purpose is manipulative, and the character doesn't speak the conclusions of the show.

4. This phrase is from Whedon's audio commentary of "Welcome to the Hellmouth" from the season 1 DVD set; his point is actually that Anthony Stewart Head brings so much more than the predictable "boring exposition guy" to the role of Giles.

5. "Welcome to the Hellmouth," *Buffy the Vampire Slayer*, 1.1.

6. The episodes "Bad Girls" and "Consequences" in season 3, where Faith kills a human, and the episode "Dead Things" in season 6, when Buffy believes she kills a human, deal with this distinction. While killing vampires is both necessary and ethically right, killing humans is always considered morally wrong on the show. The human soul seems to be what makes the difference.

7. "Never Kill a Boy on a First Date," *Buffy the Vampire Slayer*, 1.5.

8. "Nightmares," *Buffy the Vampire Slayer*, 1.10.

9. "School Hard," *Buffy the Vampire Slayer*, 2.3.

10. "Lie to Me," *Buffy the Vampire Slayer*, 2.7.

11. "Angel," *Buffy the Vampire Slayer*, 1.7.

12. "Amends," *Buffy the Vampire Slayer*, 3.10.

13. "Becoming: Part One" *Buffy the Vampire Slayer*, 2.21.

14. The interpretation of Spike's behavior as selfish in season 5 does hold up for the most part. Vampires throughout the run of the show are different based on their human personalities. Spike, even as a human, was defined by his helpless love for women, and that trait spills over into his vampire identity. His love for Drusilla in season 2 was considered by The Judge as a "human weakness," and so his love for Buffy isn't at all out of character. While season 5 paints him from time to time as sacrificially noble, it could be explained as selfishness in doing whatever he can to win Buffy's love rather than acting out of genuine self-sacrifice. Either way, in season 6, the writers clarify how viewers are supposed to view Spike and his inability to do good without a soul.

15. "Beneath You," *Buffy the Vampire Slayer*, 7.2.

16. See Rhonda Wilcox, in her chapter "Pain as Bright as Steel: Mythic Striving and Light as Pain" in *Why Buffy Matters* for an excellent analysis of light symbolism in the show.

17. See Gregory J. Sakal for a good analysis of Spike's "conversion" in his essay, "No Big Win: Themes of Sacrifice, Salvation, and Redemption."

18. "Restless," *Buffy the Vampire Slayer*, 4.22.

19. Joss Whedon quoted in Longworth, *TV Creators*, 220.

20. "Welcome to the Hellmouth," *Buffy the Vampire Slayer*, 1.1.

21. "Once More, with Feeling," *Buffy the Vampire Slayer*, 6.7.

22. Ibid. and "The Gift," *Buffy the Vampire Slayer*, 5.22.

23. "Prophecy Girl," *Buffy the Vampire Slayer*, 1.12.
24. "Becoming: Part One," *Buffy the Vampire Slayer*, 2.21.
25. "Intervention," *Buffy the Vampire Slayer*, 5.18.
26. "Grave," *Buffy the Vampire Slayer*, 6.22.
27. Forgiveness is treated as connected to love but also as an individual theme. In season 2's "I Only Have Eyes for You," Giles says, "To forgive is an act of compassion, Buffy. It's not done because people deserve it. It's done because they need it." We can see the necessity of forgiveness throughout the show in a large-scale way through the characters' dealings with Angel/Angelus, with Spike, and with Willow after season 6. We can see forgiveness in smaller ways in multiple characters and plot-arcs.
28. "Amends," *Buffy the Vampire Slayer*, 3.10.
29. In an interview with *SFX* magazine, Joss Whedon suggested this line from "Amends" as a possibility when asked about the best line he'd ever written ("Joss Whedon Answers 100 Questions").
30. "Amends," *Buffy the Vampire Slayer*, 3.10.
31. Ibid.
32. "The Freshman," *Buffy the Vampire Slayer*, 4.1.
33. "Blood Ties," *Buffy the Vampire Slayer*, 5.13.
34. "Dirty Girls," *Buffy the Vampire Slayer*, 7.18.
35. "Conversations with Dead People," *Buffy the Vampire Slayer*, 7.7.
36. As Xander sings in "Once More, with Feeling," backpedaling from his ill-chosen suggestion of evil witches causing the musical chaos: "Which is ridiculous 'cause witches they were persecuted, Wicca good and love the earth and woman power and I'll be over here."
37. "Hush," *Buffy the Vampire Slayer*, 4.10.
38. "Chosen," *Buffy the Vampire Slayer*, 7.22.
39. Tanya Krzywinska explores the use of witchcraft and magic on the show in "Hubble-Bubble, Herbs, and Grimoires: Magic, Manichaeanism, and Witchcraft in *Buffy*."
40. Playden also claims Angel's acknowledgment of his sin and search for redemption "demonstrates the limitations of the orthodox Christian ideas by which Angel the character then measures his conduct" ("'What You Are, What's to Come,'" 136). I find this part of her argument less convincing; I'd argue that it instead shows the limitations of a Christian worldview lacking in grace.
41. Brian Wall and Michael Zyrd point toward this idea in their essay, "Vampire Dialectics: Knowledge, Institutions and Labour." They argue that the "lack of mythological coherence" in *Buffy the Vampire Slayer* and *Angel* implies a "diverse and mixed universe in which multiple and shifting regimes of knowledge are aligned with salutarily multiple and shifting ethical domains" (62). Jana Reiss argues that "Buffy offers Chris-

tian symbols, Buddhist themes, a generous helping of Wiccan ethics, and some sprinkled references to Judaism, among other traditions" (*What Would Buffy Do?* xvi). James Lawler makes an argument about the multi-dimensional universe in *Buffy*, coming to different conclusions about how the show creates a picture of "human life between two worlds" ("Between Heavens and Hells," 110).

42. Whedon quoted in an interview with Emily Nussbaum, "Must See Metaphysics," *New York Times*, September 22, 2002, 56.

43. Whedon quoted in The AV Club interview with Tasha Robinson, "Joss Whedon," *The Onion*, September 5, 2001.

Chapter 5: Sookie Stackhouse

1. Harris, *Dead and Gone*, 93.
2. Ibid., *Dead Until Dark*, 1.
3. Ibid., 2.
4. Ibid., 252.
5. Ibid., 5.
6. Ibid., 92.
7. Ibid., 49.
8. Ibid., 53.
9. Ibid., 208.
10. Harris, *Dead as a Doornail*, 227.
11. Harris, *Dead Until Dark*, 16.
12. Harris, *Club Dead*, 5.
13. Harris, *Definitely Dead*, 12.
14. Harris, *Living Dead in Dallas*, 135.
15. Ibid., 126.
16. Ibid., 153.
17. Ibid., 157.
18. Harris, *Dead Until Dark*, 13.
19. Harris, *Living Dead in Dallas*, 96.
20. Harris, *Dead Until Dark*, 72.
21. A good example to show the contrast is the scene from season 3 of *Buffy* in the episode "Graduation Day: Part Two." To save Angel's life, Buffy convinces Angel to drink her blood. The scene is clearly ero-tized—emphasizing the physical and emotional intimacy between Buffy and Angel—but they don't actually have sex. Anne Rice's vampires are actually incapable of having sex, so feeding takes the place of sex for them. In Harris's novels, the sex act tends to be dominant and the drinking of blood is an additional part of the sex.
22. Harris, *Dead Until Dark*, 197.
23. Harris, *From Dead to Worse*, 34.

24. Harris, *Dead Until Dark*, 265.
25. Ibid., 33.
26. Ibid., 167.
27. Harris, *Dead to the World*, 260.
28. Harris, *Dead and Gone*, 118.
29. Ibid., 119.
30. Ibid., 155.
31. Harris, *From Dead to Worse*, 271.
32. "Strange Love," *True Blood*, 1.1.
33. "The First Taste," *True Blood*, 1.2.
34. "Mine," *True Blood*, 1.3.
35. "Escape from Dragon House," *True Blood*, 1.4.
36. Alan Ball quoted in Ausiello, "True Blood Finale Postmortem with Alan Bell," *Entertainment Weekly*, September 14, 2009.
37. "Nothing But the Blood," *True Blood*, 2.1.
38. "Frenzy," *True Blood*, 2.11.
39. "Beyond Here Lies Nothin'," *True Blood*, 2.12.

Chapter 6: Stephenie Meyer's Twilight Saga

1. Marc E. Shaw has a good article about Meyer's Mormonism and the Twilight Saga titled "For the Strength of Bella? Meyer, Vampires, and Mormonism."
2. Meyer, *New Moon*, 36.
3. Meyer, *Twilight*, 19.
4. Ibid., 260.
5. Meyer, *New Moon*, 307.
6. Meyer, *Twilight*, 135.
7. Ibid., 337.
8. Ibid., 93.
9. Meyer, *New Moon*, 10.
10. Ibid., 35.
11. Ibid., 37.
12. Meyer, *Twilight*, 11.
13. Ibid., 22.
14. Ibid., 45.
15. Ibid., 88.
16. Ibid., 266.
17. Ibid., 310.
18. This contrast seems to be intentional. In *Eclipse*, Jacob says, "I was the natural path your life would have taken. . . . If the world was the way it was supposed to be, if there were no monsters and no magic" (599).
19. Meyer, *Breaking Dawn*, 23.

20. Another common discussion regarding Edward and Bella's relationship in the books is whether or not it mirrors an abusive relationship. Edward emotionally devours Bella, controlling her actions and her other relationships to such an extent that she feels her whole life is about him—typical characteristics of an emotionally abusive relationship. Rebecca Housel's article "The 'Real' Danger: Fact vs. Fiction for the Girl Audience" goes into this reading of the novels in detail. Whether or not it is abusive, I would argue Bella and Edward's relationship certainly seems at very least unhealthy.

21. Meyer, *Twilight*, 474.

22. Meyer, *Eclipse*, 269.

23. Beth Felker Jones, in her Christian reading of the Twilight books, *Touched by a Vampire*, makes an excellent point about how Meyer portrays sex as dangerous—in a way that heightens the excitement associated with it but contradicts the purpose of sex as established by God.

24. Meyer, *Breaking Dawn*, 190.

25. Ibid., 420.

26. Ibid., 524.

27. Naomi Zack, in her article "Bella Swan and Sarah Palin: All the Old Myths Are *Not* True," argues that *Twilight* is all about a woman "having it all"—fulfilling every Western idea of romantic love and success—and it's easy to see how the novel works out that dynamic.

28. Meyer, *Breaking Dawn*, 718.

29. Beth Felker Jones argues that Meyer's depiction of family is in keeping with the Mormon concept of the link between "eternal hope" and family. She claims that Mormons see the family structure as the "basic unit of eternity," and this can be seen in the idealization of the Cullen family in the Twilight Saga (*Touched by a Vampire*, 88).

30. Meyer, *Twilight*, 195.

31. While much of the novel looks like a melodramatic, unrealistic depiction of an adolescent fantasy about love, Meyer does not want us to think that. Bella's mother, Renee, seems to impose Meyer's interpretation on the story as evidence that we're not supposed to read Bella as an infatuated teenager, although her actions nearly always come across as such. Renee says in *Breaking Dawn*, "You've never been a teenager, sweetie. You know what's best for *you*" (19). The novels don't work unless we believe Bella's love for Edward to be deep and genuine and not melodramatic fantasy.

32. Meyer, *Twilight*, 251.

33. Meyer, *New Moon*, 69.

34. Ibid., 340.

35. Meyer, *Eclipse*, 29.

36. Meyer, *Breaking Dawn*, 319.
37. Fosl and Fosl, *"Vampire-Dämmerung,"* 75.

Chapter 7: Vampire Sinners

1. *From Dusk Till Dawn*, DVD, directed by Richard Rodriquez.
2. *Dracula*, DVD, directed by Tod Browning.
3. *Dracula's Daughter*, DVD, directed by Lambert Hillyer.
4. Ibid.
5. *Son of Dracula*, DVD, directed by Robert Siodmak.
6. *House of Dracula*, DVD, directed by Erle C. Kenton.
7. Harris, *Dead Until Dark*, 72.
8. *Underworld: Evolution*, DVD, directed by Len Wiseman.
9. "The Embraced," *Kindred: The Embraced*, 1.1.

Chapter 8: Vampire Saviors

1. Yarbro, *Hôtel Transylvania*, 62.
2. Ibid.
3. "City of," *Angel*, 1.1.
4. Ibid.
5. "For I Have Sinned," *Forever Knight*, 1.3.
6. Ibid.
7. "Somnambulist," *Angel*, 1.11.
8. "Dear Boy," *Angel*, 2.5.
9. "Shiny Happy People," *Angel*, 4.18.
10. "Magic Bullet," *Angel*, 4.19.
11. "Peace Out," *Angel*, 4.21.
12. "Last Knight," *Forever Knight*, 3.22.
13. Kenyon, *Night Pleasures*, 44.
14. Ibid., 39.
15. Ibid., 61.
16. Ibid., 109.
17. Ibid., 125.
18. Ibid., 381.
19. Ibid., 2.
20. *Let the Right One In*, DVD, directed by Tomas Alfredson.
21. Ibid.
22. Hamilton, *Guilty Pleasures*, 59.
23. Ibid.
24. Ibid., 266.
25. Hamilton, *Harlequin*, 8.

Bibliography

Anderson, Wendy Love. "Prophecy Girl and the Powers That Be: The Philosophy of Religion in the Buffyverse." In *Buffy the Vampire Slayer and Philosophy: Fear and Trembling in Sunnydale*, edited by James B. South, 212–26. Chicago: Open Court, 2003.

Angel: Seasons 1–5. DVD. Created by David Greenwalt and Joss Whedon. Twentieth Century Fox Home Videos, 2007.

Arata, Stephen D. "The Occidental Tourist: *Dracula* and the Anxiety of Reverse Colonization." *Victorian Studies* 33, no. 4 (1990): 621–45. Revised and reprinted in Arata's *Fictions of Loss in the Victorian Fin de Siècle*. Cambridge: Cambridge University Press, 1996.

Auerbach, Nina. *Our Vampires, Ourselves*. Chicago: University of Chicago Press, 1997.

Ausiello, Michael. "*True Blood* Finale Postmortem with Alan Bell." The Ausiello Files. *Entertainment Weekly*. September 14, 2009. http://ausiellofiles.ew.com/2009/09/14/exclusive-true-blood-finale-postmortem-with-alan-ball/.

Belford, Barbara. *Bram Stoker: A Biography of the Author of Dracula*. New York: Knopf, 1996.

Benefiel, Candace R. "Blood Relations: The Gothic Perversion of the Nuclear Family in Anne Rice's *Interview with the Vampire*." *Journal of Popular Culture* 38, no. 2 (2004): 261–73.

Bentley, Christopher. "The Monster in the Bedroom: Sexual Symbolism in Bram Stoker's Dracula." *Literature and Psychology* 22 (1972): 27–34. Reprinted in *Dracula: The Vampire and the Critics,* edited by Margaret L. Carter, 25–34. Ann Arbor, MI: UMI Research Press, 1988.

Bierman, Joseph S. "Dracula: Prolonged Childhood Illness, and the Oral Triad." *American Imago* 29, no. 2 (1972): 186–98.

Blade. DVD. Directed by Stephen Norrington. 1998. New Line Home Video, 1998.

Buffy the Vampire Slayer: The Complete Series. DVD. Created by Joss Wheden. Twentieth Century Fox Home Video, 2005.

Byers, Thomas B. "Good Men and Monsters: The Defenses of *Dracula*." *Literature and Psychology* 31, no. 4 (1981): 24–31. Reprinted in *Dracula: The Vampire and the Critics,* edited by Margaret L. Carter, 149–58. Ann Arbor, MI: UMI Research Press, 1988.

Coulardeau, Jacques. "The Vision of Religion in Francis Ford Coppola's *Bram Stoker's Dracula.*" In *Post/modern Dracula: From Victorian Themes to Postmodern Praxis*, edited by John S. Bak, 123–39. Newcastle, UK: Cambridge Scholars, 2007.

Craft, Christopher. "'Kiss Me with Those Red Lips': Gender and Inversion in Bram Stoker's *Dracula*." *Representations* 8 (1984): 107–33. Revised and reprinted in *Another Kind of Love: Male Homosexual Desire in English Discourse, 1850–1920*, by Christopher Craft. Berkeley: University of California Press, 1994. Also reprinted in *Dracula: The Vampire and the Critics,* edited by Margaret L. Carter, 167–94. Ann Arbor, MI: UMI Research Press, 1988.

Crişan, Marius. "The Models for Castle Dracula in Stoker's Sources on Transylvania." *Journal of Dracula Studies* 10 (2008). http://www.blooferland.com/drc.

Dracula. DVD. Directed by Tod Browning. 1931. Universal Studios, 2004.

Dracula's Daughter. DVD. Directed by Lambert Hillyer. 1936. Universal Studios, 2005.

Erickson, Gregory. "'Sometimes You Need A Story': American Christianity, Vampires, and *Buffy*." In *Fighting the Forces: What's at Stake in* Buffy the Vampire Slayer, edited by Rhonda V. Wilcox and David Lavery, 108–19. Lanham, MD: Rowman and Littlefield, 2002.

Forever Knight: The Trilogy. DVD. Directed by Allan Kroeker. Sony Pictures, 2006.

Fosl, Peter S., and Eli Fosl. "*Vampire-Dämmerung*: What Can *Twilight* Tell Us about God?" In *Twilight and Philosophy: Vampires, Vegetarians, and the Pursuit of Immortality,* edited by Rebecca Housel and J. Jeremy Wisknewski, 63–78. Hoboken, NJ: Wiley, 2009.

From Dusk Till Dawn. DVD. Directed by Robert Rodriguez. 1996. Dimension Films, 2000.

Gelder, Ken. *Reading the Vampire*. New York: Routledge, 1994.

Gordon, Joan and Veronica Hollinger, ed. *Blood Read: The Vampire as Metaphor in Contemporary Culture*. Philadelphia: University of Pennsylvania Press, 1997.

Griffin, Gail B. "'Your Girls That You All Love Are Mine': *Dracula* and the Victorian Male Sexual Imagination." *International Journal of Women's Studies* 3 (1980): 454–65. Reprinted in *Dracula: The Vampire and the Critics,* edited by Margaret L. Carter, 137–48. Ann Arbor, MI: UMI Research Press, 1988.

Hamilton, Laurell K. *Blood Noir*. New York: Berkeley Books, 2008.

———. *Guilty Pleasures*. New York: Ace Books, 1993.

———. *The Harlequin*. New York: Berkeley Books, 2007.

———. *Skin Trade*. New York: Berkeley Books, 2009.

Harris, Charlaine. *All Together Dead*. New York: Ace Books, 2007.

———. *Club Dead*. New York: Ace Books, 2003.

———. *Dead and Gone*. New York: Ace Books, 2009.

———. *Dead as a Doornail*. New York: Ace Books, 2005.

———. *Dead to the World*. New York: Ace Books, 2004.

———. *Dead Until Dark*. New York: Ace Books, 2001.

———. *Definitely Dead*. New York: Ace Books, 2006.

―――. *From Dead to Worse.* New York: Ace Books, 2008.

―――. *Living Dead in Dallas.* New York: Ace Books, 2002.

Hood, Gwenyth. "Sauron and Dracula." *Mythlore* 52 (1987): 11–17. Reprinted in *Dracula: The Vampire and the Critics,* edited by Margaret L. Carter, 215–30. Ann Arbor, MI: UMI Research Press, 1988.

House of Dracula. DVD. Directed by Erle C. Kenton. 1945. Universal Studios, 2004.

Housel, Rebecca. "The 'Real' Danger: Fact vs. Fiction for the Girl Audience." In *Twilight and Philosophy: Vampires, Vegetarians, and the Pursuit of Immortality,* edited by Rebecca Housel and J. Jeremy Wisknewski, 177–92. Hoboken, NJ: Wiley, 2009.

Humphries-Brooks, Stephenson. "The Body and the Blood of Eternal UnDeath." *Journal of Religion and Popular Culture* 6 (Spring 2004). http://www.usask.ca/relst/jrpc/art6-dracula.html.

Ingebretsen, Edward J. "Anne Rice: Raising Holy Hell, Harlequin Style." In *The Gothic World of Anne Rice,* edited by Gary Hoppenstand and Ray B. Browne, 91–108. Bowling Green, OH: Bowling Green State University Popular Press, 1994.

Jones, Beth Felker. *Touched by a Vampire: Discovering the Hidden Messages in the Twilight Saga.* Colorado Springs: Multnomah, 2009.

"Joss Whedon Answers 100 Questions." *SFX* magazine. Reprinted in *Slayage.com.* February 20, 2003. June 20, 2003. http://www.slayage.com/news/030220-joss100qs.html.

Kenyon, Sherrilyn. *Night Pleasures.* Large Print edition. Prince Frederick, MD: Recorded Books, 2004.

Kindred: The Embraced: The Complete Vampire Collection. DVD. Created by John Leekley. 1996. Republic Studios, 2001.

King, Neal. "Brownskirts: Facism, Christianity, and the Eternal Demon." In *Buffy the Vampire Slayer and Philosophy: Fear and Trembling in Sunnydale,* edited by James B South, 197–211. Chicago: Open Court, 2003.

Kirtley, Bacil F. "*Dracula,* the Monastic Chronicles and Slavic Folklore." *Midwest Folklore* 6, no. 3 (1956): 133–39. Reprinted in *Dracula: The Vampire and the Critics,* edited by Margaret L. Carter, 11–18. Ann Arbor, MI: UMI Research Press, 1988.

Krzywinska, Tanya. "Hubble-Bubble, Herbs, and Grimoires: Magic, Manichaeanism, and Witchcraft in *Buffy*." In *Fighting the Forces: What's at Stake in* Buffy the Vampire Slayer, edited by Rhonda B. Wilcox and David Lavery, 178–94. Lanham, MD: Rowman and Littlefield, 2002.

Lawler, James. "Between Heavens and Hells: The Multidimensional Universe in Kant and *Buffy the Vampire Slayer*." In *Buffy the Vampire Slayer and Philosophy: Fear and Trembling in Sunnydale*, edited by James B. South, 103–16. Chicago: Open Court, 2003.

Let the Right One In. DVD. Directed by Tomas Alfredson. 2008. Magnolia Home Entertainment, 2009.

Liberman, Terri R. "Eroticism as Moral Fulcrum in Rice's Vampire Chronicles." In *The Gothic World of Anne Rice*, edited by Gary Hoppenstand and Ray B. Browne, 109–21. Bowling Green, OH: Bowling Green State University Popular Press, 1994.

Lindqvist, John Ajvide. *Let the Right One In.* Translated by Ebba Segerberg. New York: Thomas Dunne Books, 2007.

Longworth, James L., Jr. *TV Creators: Conversations with America's Top Producers of Television Drama.* Vol. 2, The Television Series. Syracuse, NY: Syracuse University Press, 2002.

McNally, Raymond T. and Radu Florescu. *In Search of Dracula: A True History of Dracula and Vampire Legends.* Greenwich, CT: New York Graphic Society, 1972.

Meyer, Stephenie. *Breaking Dawn.* New York: Little, Brown, 2008.

———. *Eclipse.* New York: Little, Brown, 2007.

———. *New Moon.* New York: Little, Brown, 2006.

———. *Twilight.* New York: Little, Brown, 2005.

Moses, Michael Valdez. "The Irish Vampire: *Dracula*, Parnell, and the Troubled Dreams of Nationhood." *Journal x* 2, no. 1 (Autumn 1997): 67–111.

Nandris, Grigore. "The Historical Dracula: The Theme of His Legend in the Western and in Eastern Literatures of Europe." *Comparative Literature Studies* 3, no. 4 (1966): 367–96.

Nussbaum, Emily. "Must See Metaphysics." *New York Times*, September 22, 2002, late edition, sec. 6. Online edition, http://www.nytimes.com/2002/09/22/magazine/must-see-metaphysics.html.

Pateman, Matthew. *The Aesthetics of Culture in* Buffy the Vampire Slayer. Jefferson, NC: McFarland, 2006.

Playden, Zoe-Jane. "'What You Are, What's to Come': Feminisms, Citizenship and the Divine." In *Reading the Vampire Slayer: An Unofficial Critical Companion to* Buffy *and* Angel, edited by Roz Kaveney, 120–47. London: Tauris Parke, 2002.

Raible, Christopher Gist. "Dracula: Christian Heretic." *Christian Century* 96, no. 4 (1979): 103–4. Reprinted in *Dracula: The Vampire and the Critics,* edited by Margaret L. Carter, 105–7. Ann Arbor, MI: UMI Research Press, 1988.

Ramsland, Katherine. *Prism of the Night: A Biography of Anne Rice.* New York: Plume Books, 1992.

———. *Vampire Companion: The Official Guide to Anne Rice's The Vampire Chronicles.* New York: Ballantine, 1993.

Reiss, Jana. *What Would Buffy Do? The Vampire Slayer as Spiritual Guide.* San Francisco: Jossey-Bass, 2004.

Rice, Anne. *Blackwood Farm.* New York: Alfred A. Knopf, 2002.

———. *Blood and Gold.* New York: Alfred A. Knopf, 2001.

———. *Blood Canticle.* New York: Alfred A. Knopf, 2003.

———. *Christ the Lord: Out of Egypt.* New York: Alfred A. Knopf, 2005.

———. *Christ the Lord: Road to Cana.* New York: Alfred A. Knopf, 2008.

———. *Interview with the Vampire.* New York: Alfred A. Knopf, 1976.

———. *Memnoch the Devil.* New York: Alfred A. Knopf, 1995.

———. *Merrick.* New York: Alfred A. Knopf, 2000.

———. *The Queen of the Damned.* New York: Alfred A. Knopf, 1988.

———. *The Tale of the Body Thief.* New York: Alfred A. Knopf, 1992.

———. *The Vampire Armand.* New York: Alfred A. Knopf, 1998.

———. *The Vampire Lestat.* New York: Ballantine, 1985.

Richardson, Maurice. "The Psychoanalysis of Ghost Stories." *Twentieth Century* 166 (1959): 419–31.

Rickels, Laurence A. *Vampire Lectures*. Minneapolis: University of Minnesota Press, 1999.

Riley, Michael. *Conversations with Anne Rice*. New York: Ballantine Books, 1996.

Roberts, Bette B. *Anne Rice*. Twayne United States Authors Series. Edited by Frank Day. New York: Twayne, 1994.

Robinson, Tasha. "Joss Whedon." Interview with Joss Whedon. The AV Club. *The Onion*, September 5, 2001. http://www.avclub.com/articles/joss-whedon,13730/. Web exclusive version, http://www.avclub.com/articles/joss-whedon-web-exclusive,13729/.

Ronay, Gabriel. *The Truth about Dracula*. New York: Stein and Day, 1972.

Roth, Phyllis A. "Suddenly Sexual Women in Bram Stoker's *Dracula*." *Literature and Psychology* 27 (1977): 113–21. Reprinted in *Dracula: The Vampire and the Critics*, edited by Margaret L. Carter, 57–68. Ann Arbor, MI: UMI Research Press, 1988.

Rout, Kathleen. "Who Do You Love? Anne Rice's Vampires and Their Moral Transition." *Journal of Popular Culture* 36, no. 3 (2003): 473–79.

Sakal, Gregory J. "No Big Win: Themes of Sacrifice, Salvation, and Redemption." In *Buffy the Vampire Slayer and Philosophy: Fear and Trembling in Sunnydale*, edited by James B. South, 239–53. Chicago: Open Court, 2003.

Schmitt, Cannon. "Mother Dracula: Orientalism, Degeneration, and the Anglo-Irish National Subjectivity at the Fin de Siècle." In *Irishness and (Post)Modernism*, edited by John S. Rickard, 25–43. London: Associated University Press, 1994.

Shafer, Aileen Chris. "Let Us Prey: Religious Codes and Ritual in *The Vampire Lestat*." In *The Gothic World of Anne Rice*, edited by Gary Hoppenstand and Ray B. Browne, 149–61. Bowling Green, OH: Bowling Green State University Popular Press, 1994.

Shaw, Marc E. "For the Strength of Bella? Meyer, Vampires, and Mormonism." In *Twilight and Philosophy: Vampires, Vegetarians, and the Pursuit of Immortality*, edited by Rebecca Housel and J. Jeremy Wisknewski, 227–36. Hoboken, NJ: Wiley, 2009.

Son of Dracula. DVD. Directed by Robert Siodmak. 1943. Universal Studios, 2004.

Stevenson, John Allen. "The Vampire in the Mirror: The Sexuality of *Dracula*." *Publications of the Modern Language Association* (*PMLA*) 103 (1988): 139–49.

Stoker, Bram. *Dracula*. Edited by John Paul Riquelme. Case Studies in Contemporary Criticism. Boston: Bedford/St. Martin's Press, 2002.

True Blood. Seasons 1–3. Television program. HBO, 2008–2010. Directed by Alan Ball.

Underworld. DVD. Directed by Len Wiseman. 2003. Sony Pictures, 2004.

Underworld: Evolution. DVD. Directed by Len Wiseman. 2006. Sony Pictures, 2006.

Vampire Hunter D. DVD. Directed by Toyou Ashida and Carl Macek. 1985. Urban Vision, 2000.

Wall, Brian and Michael Zyrd. "Vampire Dialectics: Knowledge, Institutions and Labour." In *Reading the Vampire Slayer: An Unofficial Critical Companion to* Buffy *and* Angel, edited by Roz Kaveney, 53–77. London: Tauris Parke, 2002.

Weissman, Judith. "Women as Vampires: *Dracula* as a Victorian Novel." *Midwest Quarterly* 18 (1977): 392–405. Reprinted in *Dracula: The Vampire and the Critics,* edited by Margaret L. Carter, 69–78. Ann Arbor, MI: UMI Research Press, 1988.

Whedon, Joss. "Welcome to the Hellmouth." Audio commentary. *Buffy the Vampire Slayer—The Complete First Season*. DVD. 1997. Twentieth Century Fox Home Video, 2002.

Wilcox, Rhonda V. *Why Buffy Matters: The Art of* Buffy the Vampire Slayer. London: I. B. Tauris, 2005.

Wolf, Leonard. *A Dream of Dracula: In Search of the Living Dead*. New York: Little, Brown, 1972.

Wood, Martin J. "New Life for an Old Tradition: Anne Rice and Vampire Literature." In *The Blood Is the Life: Vampires in Literature*, edited by Leonard G. Heldreth and Mary Pharr, 59–78. Bowling Green, OH: Bowling Green State University Popular Press, 1999.

Worley, Lloyd. "Anne Rice's Protestant Vampires." In *The Blood Is the Life: Vampires in Literature*, edited by Leonard G. Heldreth and Mary Pharr, 79–92. Bowling Green, OH: Bowling Green State University Popular Press, 1999.

Yarbro, Chelsea Quinn. *Hôtel Transylvania: A Novel of Forbidden Love*. New York: St. Martin's Press, 1978.

Zack, Naomi. "Bella Swan and Sarah Palin: All the Old Myths Are *Not* True." In *Twilight and Philosophy: Vampires, Vegetarians, and the Pursuit of Immortality,* edited by Rebecca Housel and J. Jeremy Wisknewski, 121–30. Hoboken, NJ: Wiley, 2009.

Index

addiction, 97, 144, 146
agape, 70–71
alcoholism, 97, 99
Alfredson, Tomas, 152
alienation, social, 113
allegory, *Dracula* as, 27
Amano, Yoshitaka, 132
ambition, 133, 138
Angel (TV program), 143, 144–45,
   146–48, 159, 164
angels, 34, 108, 115–16
anger, 157
angst, 38–39, 51
Anita Blake, Vampire Hunter series, 83
apocalypse, 175n2
atheism, 80
atonement, 101, 144, 145
Auerbach, Nina, 5, 167n2(1)

Ball, Alan, 99
baptism, 162
Bathory, Elisabeth, 168n3
beauty, 105, 106, 113, 156
Bible
   in *Dracula*, 18
   and sin, 63
Bierman, Joseph, 169n5
Blackwood Farm (novel), 50

Blade (film), 132–34
blood, 16, 25, 128
   of animals, 37
   of Christ, 25, 26, 49
   and communion, 26, 142
   drinking of, 3, 109, 110, 112, 115, 129,
      144, 151, 153
   and sex, 6, 90–93, 137, 138, 157, 178n21
   symbolism of, 57–58
Blood Canticle (novel), 53, 108
Blood Noir (novel), 157
bloody sacrifice, 66, 68–70
Breaking Dawn (novel), 107, 109, 112,
   116, 118–19, 120, 122
British Empire, 169n5
Browning, Tod, 128
Buffy the Vampire Slayer (TV program),
   9, 57–81, 108, 134, 144, 152, 164
Buffyverse, 60, 68, 72, 76, 79

Cain, mark of, 31
Carmilla (novel), 4, 5
Catholic Church, 3, 13, 51, 86, 88
Cerulean Sins (novel), 157
"Christabel" (poem), 5
Christ figure, 101, 138
Christian iconography, 35, 58
Christianity, in *Buffy*, 74–76

Christians, and vampires, 7–9
Christian worldview, 8–10, 25, 32, 35, 45, 55, 93, 162
clan conflict, 138
Club Dead (novel), 87, 94
Coleridge, Samuel Taylor, 5
Communion, 25, 26, 49, 58, 88, 89, 161
community, 6, 135–40
consciousness, 34
control, 115
Crisan, Marius, 169n3
cross, 49, 65, 99, 107, 145, 158, 167n2(2)
    power of, 3, 21, 130, 131
    symbol of, 13–16, 27, 28–29, 146, 161
culture, 2, 7, 11, 162, 163
cynicism, 126

damnation, 26, 106, 111
Dead and Gone (novel), 82, 95, 96
Dead as a Doornail (novel), 87
Dead to the World (novel), 94
Dead Until Dark (novel), 83, 85–86, 87, 91, 93, 94, 98, 135
Definitely Dead (novel), 88
depression, 121
desire, 114–15, 130
despair, 20, 38, 39, 40, 41
devil, 38, 46–50. *See also* Satan
dhampirs. See half-vampires
Dionysus, 42–43
disability, 85, 86
discernment, 7–8
Dracula (film), 128–29
Dracula (novel), 8–9, 19–32, 58, 60–61, 76, 80, 108, 163
Dracula's Daughter (film), 129–30

Eclipse (novel), 111–12, 117, 122
Egyptians, 42
envy, 19–20
Episcopal Church, 88
eschatology, 175n2
eternal life, 25
Eucharist, 25
evil, 35, 72, 73, 127, 129–31, 133, 146–47, 155, 156, 162

faith, 16, 104, 118, 126, 127, 146, 158, 162
    and morality, 93–96
    and salvation, 29–32
family, 120–21, 180n29
fanaticism, 87–89, 93–94, 98, 99
fascism, 175n2
feeding, and sex, 89, 90–92, 178n21
Feehan, Christine, 2
feminism, 79
flesh, 50–51, 164
Florescu, Radu, 168n3
Forever Knight (TV program), 143, 144, 145–46, 148, 159
forgiveness, 58, 95, 101, 177n27
Fosl, Eli, 123
Fosl, Peter, 123
free will, 127, 134, 140, 144, 147–48, 157
    in *Buffy the Vampire Slayer*, 58, 61, 64, 85
    in Twilight Saga, 105, 108–12, 120, 122–23
    Freudian theory, 167n2(1)
From Dead to Worse (novel), 96
From Dusk Till Dawn (film), 125–27, 154–55

garlic, 3, 27
Gelder, Ken, 167n2
gender studies, 169n5
gifts, 107, 148
gluttony, 18–19
God
    existence of, 38, 40–41, 46, 76, 104
    face of, 48–49
    as incarnate, 45–51
    mercy of, 21
    power of, 29, 30
Gothic genre, 14, 16
Gordon, Joan, 167n2(1)
grace, 58, 59, 66, 72–74, 75, 164
greed, 19, 20
Greeks, 43
guilt, 9, 10, 31, 130, 132, 138–39, 162
    in Anne Rice, 34–39, 40, 43, 48, 50, 51, 54–55
    in *Buffy the Vampire Slayer*, 58, 59, 61, 62, 65

in Southern Vampire Mysteries, 84, 86, 89, 95, 101
in Twilight Saga, 109
Guilty Pleasures (novel), 155–57

half-vampires, 118, 132–34, 140
Hamilton, Laurell K., 2, 6, 83, 143, 155, 158
Harris, Charlaine, 2, 6, 10, 81–102, 134, 135, 155
heaven, 47–48, 79
hell, 47–48
hero, vampire as, 143, 149, 150, 154
Hollinger, Veronica, 167n2(1)
homosexuality, 78
Hood, Gwyneth, 168n2
Hôtel Transylvania (novel), 141–43
House of Dracula (film), 131
hypnosis, 3, 22, 30
hypocrisy, 99–100

icons, 47
image of God, 163
immortality, 117, 145–46, 151
incarnation, 45–51
Interview with the Vampire (film), 36–37
Interview with the Vampire (novel), 9, 17, 35–40, 44, 45, 51
Irish studies, 169n5
irony, 69, 126
Isis, 42
Islam, 87

Jesus Christ
blood of, 25, 26, 49
as brother, 53
face of, 52–53
humanity of, 55
work of, 164
Jordan, Neil, 36–37

Keltoi (Celts), 43
Kenyon, Sherrilyn, 2, 149–52, 154, 155
Kikuchi, Hideyuki, 132
Kindred: The Embraced (TV program), 135–36, 137–38, 139
Kirtley, Bacil, 168n3
Krzywinska, Tanya, 177n39

Last Supper, 75
Lawler, James, 178n41
Leekley, John, 135
Le Fanu, Sheridan, 4, 5
lesbianism, 78
Let the Right One In (film), 149, 152–54
Lindqvist, John Ajvide, 152
Living Dead in Dallas (novel), 88, 89, 90, 93, 100
living sacrifice, 66–68
Lord's Supper. *See* Communion
love, 59, 64, 66, 70–72, 75. *See also* romance
as predestined, 120–23
transcendent, 51–55
Lugosi, Bela, 17, 128
lust, 19, 90, 97, 131, 157

McNally, Raymond T., 168n3
Memnoch the Devil (novel), 46–50
mercy, 93, 95, 133
Merrick (novel), 45
metaphor, vampire as, 4–6, 161–62, 167n2(1)
Meyer, Stephenie, 1, 6, 10, 17, 103–23, 134, 149
morality, 6, 44, 96, 127, 135, 139, 140, 154
and faith, 93–96
Mormonism, 104, 179n1, 180n29
mortality, 110, 117, 144
Moses, 18
murder, 94, 153
Murnau, Wilhelm, 61
mystery, 113–14

Nandris, Grigore, 168n3
New Moon (novel), 111, 121
Night Pleasures (novel), 149–52
nihilism, 35, 38, 39, 41
Nosferatu (novel), 61

occult, 162
Osiris, 42
Our Vampires, Ourselves (book), 5
Out of Egypt (novel), 55

paganism, 9, 35, 42–45, 76–78
Passover, 31
pedophilia, 89
philosophy, 59
physical appearance, 16–17
Playden, Zoe-Jane, 79, 177n40
Polidori, John William, 4
postcolonialism, 169n5
postmodernism, 58, 59, 79, 147
power, 155, 157, 158, 159
prayer, 36
prejudice, 84
pride, 20, 133
psychoanalytic criticism, 169n5
psychosexual perspective, 169n5

Queen of the Damned (novel), 44–45

race, 84
Raible, Christopher Gist, 167n2(2)
Ramsland, Katherine, 172n7, 172n8
rape, 64, 80, 158
reason, scientific, 29
rebellion, 40
redemption, 6, 9, 102, 143–49, 159, 162,
    177n40
Reiss, Jana, 177n41
religion, 74
responsibility, 113, 115, 117
    for evil, 62–63
Rice, Anne, 9, 17, 33–56, 59, 76, 80, 107,
    108, 163–64
Rice, Stan, 172n7
Richardson, Maurice, 169n5
Rickel, Laurence A., 167n2
Riley, Michael, 33, 50
ritual, 69–70, 99
Road to Cana (novel), 55
Roberts, Bette R., 45
Rodriquez, Robert, 125
Rout, Kathleen, 172n6
romance, 112–18, 121–23, 149–54
Ronay, Gabriel, 168n3

sacrament, 46, 142, 172n8
sacrifice, 9, 32, 58, 59, 65, 66–71, 110,
    119, 162

sacrificial living, 73
sacrificial love, 70, 108
salvation, 16, 24, 25–26, 73–74
    by faith, 29–32
Satan, 3, 43, 142–43. *See also* devil
Savage Garden, 41–42, 54
science, 131–32, 137
secrecy, 138
secularization, 10, 74–80, 129, 162, 163
self-control, 119, 150
self-defense, 95
selfishness, 64
selflessness, 54
seven deadly sins, 18–20
sex, 5–6, 21–23, 118, 137, 138, 142,
    154–58
    and blood, 90–93
    and feeding, 89, 178n21
    and religion, 172n8
sin, 6, 10, 35, 58, 132, 143, 162–64
    in *Buffy the Vampire Slayer*, 59–66
    concept of, 102, 127, 134, 135, 140,
    158
    of humanity, 73
    vampire as symbol of, 9, 15, 16–21, 24,
    36, 127–28, 130
skepticism, 99, 147
Skin Trade (novel), 157
sleep, 107
sloth, 20
Son of Dracula (film), 130
soul, 60, 64–65, 88, 110, 121–22, 123,
    131, 151, 170n22, 176n6
    battle for, 23–24
Southern Vampire Mysteries, 81–102,
    152, 163
Spelling, Aaron, 136
spirit, and flesh, 164
spiritual torment, 9, 16
spiritual warfare, 16, 58, 162, 163
stake, 3, 24, 100, 107, 129, 170n20
Stoker, Bram, 3, 8, 13–33, 60, 168n2
suicide, 89, 116
sunlight, 105–6
superhero, vampire as, 106–8, 123
superstition, 29, 30, 44
symbols, 24–29, 35, 161–62, 171n39

syncretism, 44
synthetic blood, 84, 85, 91, 136

Tale of the Body Thief (novel), 41, 46
temptation, 6, 9, 10, 15, 84, 92, 102, 126, 131–32, 162–63
tolerance, 102
transformation
  into vampire, 23–24
  spiritual, 34
  transubstantiation, 172n8
True Blood (TV program), 8, 10, 83, 97–102
turning the other cheek, 93, 95
Twilight (film), 116
Twilight (novel), 17, 107, 114, 117, 121, 142
Twilight Saga, 1, 10, 103–23, 152, 163

Underworld films, 135–37, 138–40

Vampire Armand (novel), 52
Vampire: The Masquerade (role-playing game), 135
Vampire Hunter D (film), 132, 133–34
Vampire Lestat (novel), 40, 42–44
vampires
  characteristics of, 3
  gifts of, 107, 148
  as hero, 143, 149, 150, 154
  history of, 2–4
  as metaphor, 4–6, 161–62, 167n2(1)
  pagan roots of, 42–45
  as Protestant, 171n4
  relevance of, 163
  as sympathetic, 159
Vampyre (novel), 4
Varney the Vampire (novel), 4
vegetarians, vampires as, 104
Victorian chastity, 22
violence, 64, 84, 126, 138
virus, 84, 86

Wall, Brian, 177n41
werewolves, 122, 137
Whedon, Joss, 9, 58, 66, 80
witchcraft, 76–78, 177n39
Wolf, Leonard, 169n5
Wolf Man, 131
Wood, Martin, 171n5
worldview(s), 4, 6, 7, 29, 96, 97
  multiple, 58–59, 76, 147
  transformation of, 8
  Worley, Lloyd, 171n4
wrath, 18, 20
Wuthering Heights (novel), 122

Yarbro, Chelsea Quinn, 141, 143

Zyrd, Michael, 177n41

Acknowledgments

Ideas and inspiration for this book came to me from a number of sources. Thanks to Christina and Nathan Hitchcock for a fascinating conversation in Scotland on *Dracula* that eventually led to my main argument about vampire stories. And thanks to Lee Anna Maynard for telling me about a great new television show called *Buffy the Vampire Slayer*—the first time I ever took vampires seriously. I would also like to thank my graduate assistant, Chelsen Vicari, for her assistance in culling through research and fussing with footnotes, and my department intern, Michan Meyer, for her helpful feedback on the Anne Rice chapter. I greatly appreciate my editor, Rodney Clapp, for his guidance in shaping the project and his editorial feedback. And, finally, my love and appreciation to my family, who have spent the last year hearing and reading more about vampires than they ever wanted to know.